Awakenin

(Hope for those on the journey)

by

Chris White

Awakenings & Ripples (Hope For Those On The Journey)

Copyright © 2022 by Chris White

KDP ISBN Number : 979-8357-4454-14

....

All photos by Chris White unless otherwise stated

Front cover:
Luskentyre beach looking north

Rear cover :
1. The van on the edge of Rannoch Moor
2. Ian (inside) & Chris
3. Chris on Luskentyre Beach, Harris.
(Photo – Ian White)

Cover design and typesetting by Chris White

....

There will be a whole load more photos at the end
of the book, I hope you enjoy those too!
(But only look at them once you've finished reading the book!)

Dedications & Acknowledgements

Did you know, I actually have lots of families, which is lovely!
This book is dedicated to many of them...

My 'family' family...
To Wendy, Alan & Lesley, Simon & Helen and Emma & David.
Thank you for your unending encouragement and love, always.

My Offspring Family...
To Callum & Matthew.
Hey boys, I think about you daily. Travel light, journey well, be encouragers,
stay close to Him, seize the day, laugh lots, love you billions!

To my Loch Leven Church Family...
To Richard & Alison, Marc, Kevin, Stephen, Neil & Kath, Graham & Helen,
Pete & Jess, Lynette, Sam, and so many others...
Thank you for your beautiful welcome, your creativity, your patience with
me, your hearts of worship, your humour and laughter and deep faith –
I'm loving journeying with you all!

To my Family of Friends...
To Jon, Andy, Ian, Matt, Mark, Lynsey & Craig, Beth & Guy,
Judy, Bryn & Cath, Jim & the LSM crew, and so many more who have loved
and encouraged me through both the sleeping and waking days.
If not for you all, I would still be in such a barren place, love you x.

And to Ian & Rose...
Thank you for accepting me as I am, forgiving me when I fell, supporting me
when I was struggling, journeying with me through so many ups and downs,
and running the race with me whatever obstacles now come our way.
Love you both, you're very precious.
Ian, eight days in a campervan was an absolute pleasure!

There are undoubtedly more adventures to come!

Contents

. . . . .

1.

The Bit Where I Start

I grasp the campervan steering wheel with a white-knuckled nervousness, some apprehension, and much excitement, before glancing over to Ian.

I'm grinning widely, he smiles back.

There's a glint in our eyes, I have butterflies.

I let off the handbrake.
We're on the move!
It's *actually* happening!

We're going!
Northwards!

Little did we know of the grand adventure that was to come!

And the deep changes it would bring...

2.

Introductions...

Hello reader!

My name is Chris.

I'm fifty-two. I live in a tiny cosy cottage in the rural town of Crieff, in beautiful Perthshire, Scotland. I love horses, dogs, walking, cheese, a nice pint in a low-ceilinged pub, frosty mornings, beautiful views, empty beaches, the smell of mulled wine as Christmas approaches, reading, laughing with friends, cheesecake, faith-chat, firepits, family, and singing!

Very, very occasionally, they might all happen on the same day, which is an absolute and utter treat!

Anyway, you'll get to know me and some of my friends a whole lot better over the course of the next few hours as we journey together! I love how written text can do that! Amazing!

But first-off, thank you so much for joining me!

I'd like to welcome you to a true story.

It'll take a little bit of time.
Along the way there will be excitement and amazement.
There will probably be moments of being a bit speechless.

There may be some sadness and the odd tear, but laughter too.

And above all, there will be hope. Bucket loads.
Because all the things that happened to me, they can happen to you too! And that is *my* hope in writing, and inviting you in.

So find a comfy and cosy place to sit, and grab a mug of something hot.

Perhaps a biscuit too, or cake?
Yes, definitely cake!!
And join me.

I have much to tell you of what happened on that amazing journey, some of the extraordinary things that led up to it, and something of the great ripples that have happened since!

It was a truly remarkable time, where deep called to deep, and my life changed trajectory! And where, through tears, astonishment, and laughter, and gentle but purposeful God-moments, deep mending happened.

And I suppose, in a way, I woke up, and learned to live again!

And we will return to this journey shortly, I promise!

....

But to start with, and to appreciate the now of things, we need to spin time's arrow back and return briefly to the pre-waking days.

It won't take long, I assure you, but before we head up the road, white-knuckled in the campervan, where adventures are calling you, I need to show you something of the sleepy terrain I had wandered about in for far too long prior to that.

The terrain where, for layers of reasons, my faith journey had simply stalled.

You might be familiar with that terrain yourself.

You might actually be in that place right now. Many are.
It's way more densely populated than you might imagine.

(But don't worry, there is a Way out, there is hope, its ok.)

Let me tell you of how it all started.

Come with me, if you will...

3.

The Journeying

So I became a Christian when I was about 15yrs old.

That first awakening occurred in a wee cottage in the middle of the Loch Ard Forest, surrounded by trees and midges and the sound of the flowing stream, and April birdsong, and guitars, and people who cared, and the laughter of friends. Good days! Awesome days, in fact!

Following the teenage days of the forest encounter, my Christ-faith journey has led me to some amazing places, spaces, times, and moments.

It's brought me alongside amazing people, fellow journeyers, travellers with the same destination.

We are the procession of the ragged, the broken, the wounded and the struggling.

But these same ragged folk who I travel with are also faith-filled, hopeful, visionary, forgiven, forgiving, worshipful and encouraging.

That's the beauty of it. That's church!

So we walk together, experiencing the mending, healing, equipping, life-giving and transforming power of Father God.

It's a fabulous and miraculous process. Bit by bit being honed and changed and made and remade and blundering and striding confidently, and getting lost and frequently failing and falling, but just as often being lifted and carried and fed and watered and clothed and celebrated and changed.

It's messy. And it's marvellous!

Sometimes the journey, it's been hilarious, joy-filled, surreal, astonishing and purposeful.

Sometimes, it's felt quite ordinary.

And I'm not gonna lie, some parts of the journey have been painful, sorrow-filled, perplexing, uncertain, frustrating, shame-filled, and quite heart-breaking.

I guess that's how life is, though.
The bewildering tapestry of ups and downs.
Victories and defeats.
Summits and valleys.
Triumphs and tears.

But here's the thing….
(or one of them, at least) (I'm sure there's lots, actually)
I'd rather navigate that bewildering mix with a totally 'for-me' Saviour at my side, than be distant and cut off from Him, and trying to go it alone, in my own strength, wearing mask after mask that I'm deeply afraid to remove lest people see the real me. That IS a thing. Genuinely.

Masks.
Dreadful things.
Thankfully, with Jesus, I never need to wear one.

Why would I? He knows me. Really knows me.
And He really likes me.

He also deeply loves me for who I am, warts and all, and for who He's making me to be.
(I don't have any _actual_ warts, just so you know)
(at least I don't think so)
(I'll check later)

But I'm going to be honest.
(I'd like to think that this whole book will be)

I do, sadly, have a few masks still, and sometimes when I feel particularly journey-weary, or hurting, I might slip one on, secretly, just because, sometimes, I'm still scared that if people saw how rubbish I actually am often at living a Jesus-centred life, then they may not like me very much, or they may call me a hypocrite, or it may turn them off journeying with me, or others, you know?

Thankfully, that mask mostly stays hidden away. Mostly.
And thankfully, my current companions on the journey seem to like me as I am. The actual me. Chris.

And very thankfully, I'm discovering that it's in the honest sharing of our weaknesses that true friends become closer, and the walk is strengthened, and arms are linked ever tighter, and we continue forwards together, regardless of, despite and because of our weaknesses.

We need Jesus, and we need each other.
That's it really.

But we do get hurt though.

As I've travelled, I've discovered that being a follower of Jesus doesn't make the path smooth and straight and hazard-free, but it does ensure there's good company, a sense of purpose, and a very good guide and Shepherd who IS the WAY, and who's leading us to a clear, beautiful and welcoming homecoming at the last.

And I love that!

That's the faith-journey.

But, like I said, sometimes we get hurt, and stuff propels us into difficult and dark places.

Let me briefly tell you about just such a time...

(I've not forgotten about the campervan adventure,
by the way, we'll get there shortly!)

4.

The Hurting and the Sleep

Being a spiritual somnambulist is a strange thing.
(Now that's a phrase that might need some unpacking)
(I've just thought it up, and even I'm not entirely sure what I mean!)

A somnambulist is one who sleepwalks.
Asleep, but walking about.
And for the past ten years or so, I suppose that's an apt description for where I was in my faith-journey. I was outwardly showing many of the signs of awakeness, but inside, just...not always.

My working life from the age of 22 has consisted of working as a youth worker, a Schools Christian Worker, an Associate Pastor in an Evangelical church, working with others in church planting, working for a charity supporting youth workers on the margins, running Christian outdoor activity weekends for vulnerable teenagers, being a Youth Pastor in a church of Scotland church, working with teenagers with autism, and of late, singing in care homes, pubs and hotels, along with some street busking! (Yes, things took a very unexpected turn towards the end there!)

So I've done a whole pile of Christian church stuff over the last thirty years. For much of that, I was motivated, and eager, and focussed.

I pioneered and planned, I recruited and rallied others, I was on the ball and making a difference. I was very busy. Perhaps too busy?

But then some stuff happened.
This isn't really the place to say what, exactly.
But I got hurt, on the inside, where hurts are the hurtiest.

Hurts on the outside of us tend to be very good at getting better on their own. Which is nice. (Sometimes they do need a wee blob of Savlon to help the process)

But inside hurts, those emotional wounds that we all suffer, well, they can be devastating. Left to their own devices, these wounds can fester and rot and cause untold pain, scarring, anger, bitterness, resentment, and weariness.

...And worst of all, a *deep sadness of the heart*.

They make it so you feel like you can hardly ever trust again.
They make you overly cautious, lest the hurt happens again.
Being overly cautious means you don't let people in, you don't take any risks, you're dulled to all the beautiful things life has to offer, and consequently you can come across as cold, uninterested, or aloof. (But you're not any of those things! You're just desperate not to be hurt again!)

So you build a wall around yourself as protection against further attack and damage. And tragically, the wall keeps out all the beautiful healing possibilities too.

And so, I went into my cave.

My response to the hurt was to shut out many of the very people who loved me and wanted to help me through. I couldn't help it. I was too upset and broken and numbed to take a different path. I let the hurt take root, and it flourished in the soil of my pain and self-pity, and rather than looking outward and upward to the Great Comforter, I sadly just caved in on myself. It's very easy to do.

And slowly, like the coming of the darkness at the twilight end of the day, the sun set, the Son was pushed away, I didn't understand why things had happened the way they did, I blamed Father God, and blamed myself.

And so it was that I slipped into a long, dulled, waking sleep.
I was a spiritual somnambulist.

I made some dreadfully poor choices during those years.
I hurt myself. I hurt others. I know I hurt Father God.
I still live with some of the consequences.
It wasn't nice. At all.

I never stopped believing the Son was there.
I just didn't have the wherewithal to reach up, open the curtains and let His light in.

I still did a wee bit of churching, and worship leading, now and again. I clung on, but I didn't feel rooted anywhere in particular. I drifted. And I tried to convince myself that it was all fine. But I knew it wasn't.

And I meandered like a river as it wends its way in great sweeping curves along a wide valley floor. I wandered, somewhat lost, and yet, I knew very deep down that Father God had a hold of me.

He still used me in my weak state to encourage others, which was a very humbling and beautiful thing to experience, but I just didn't know how to get out of that forlorn landscape, that Vale of Tears.

At times, I didn't even want to leave.
The valley of sadness became home.
And everyone needs a place to call home.

Sometimes it became like a patchwork cloak, made up of all my disappointments, and I would foolishly wrap myself up in it to try and keep warm. But disappointments are not the fuel that warms our hearts.

Sometimes it felt like there was never going to be a way out, or through.

Sometimes I simply didn't care.

Other times I cared deeply and fiercely and hugely.
And I would weep.

Father was very gracious to me in this time.
Very gentle. Unbelievably kind.

He held me delicately like the fragile pieces of broken pottery that I was. He gathered the pieces together and lovingly kept them, like precious treasure, waiting patiently until the time was right for the waking and the mending.

He loved me unconditionally, and walked with me constantly, even though I couldn't always see it at the time.

He also surrounded me with some very dear and beautiful friends, dotted all around the U.K, and colleagues and family, some of whom were also in the Vale of Tears, but there was a strength in numbers, and I'm so very grateful for the loving company of those who walked with me, and I with them.

What a gift that was and still is.

God is good.
All the time.

That was the sleeping.

And then, quite unexpectedly, last year, something changed!

5.

The Waking

It's an odd thing, isn't it, waking up.

You're aware of it only in hazy half-light.
The conscious is momentarily perplexed and unsure.
There's mystery as it tries to make sense of sounds and
textures and the space around.

And then, after some time of adjusting, you open your eyes.
And instinctively blink at the stream of light, intense and rich.
And yawn away the high-tide detritus of the dream-state.
And stretch, reigniting movement in stilled muscles.

And you stir.
You begin to stir.
You're waking….

And so it was that in the autumn of 2021, my days, months,
and years of sleepy hibernation came to an end. A surprising
end, in fact!

A surprising, and exciting and curious and beautiful end.

Something was afoot!

Warmth was seeping in!

Aslan was on the move and the icy land of Narnia was starting to thaw! The season of idling was drawing to a very welcome close.

I can't say for sure how, or when, or why exactly it happened as it did. It may have been that coming out of the pandemic had a part to play. It may have been that the shape of my routine had changed, and that was a good thing. I was making better choices, those surely helped.

But thinking about it now, I'm sure it was actually all down to Father's hand, and His timing.

So in the autumn of 2021, there was a sea change.

It wasn't a thunderbolt from the skies or blinding flash of light moment. But, as is often the way with Father, it was a gentle opening of the curtains and easing of the burden.

I began to feel lighter.
The weariness was passing.
I was waking up.

It was the long exhale during a storm when you know the worst has passed, and it's going to be ok. And in looking back through my journals of that time, I see that I began to pray again for other people too. I was starting to look upward at last. Upward and outward.

It's amazing how the direction of our gaze can utterly shape how we feel and who we are and where we're going.
Where is your gaze turned to in these days?
My advice - upward and outward is good.

And I started to feel a longing, a growing hunger that I'd not felt in a good while.

It felt good to feel hungry.
Feeling hungry means you're still alive.

And alive is good!

And my new longing was for something of the Journey once again. And reconnecting with others enroute.

I'd been away and asleep too long.

I missed Father.
And I missed His voice and His company.

It really was time to waken,

   breathe deeply,

     open my eyes,

       and live again!

6.

The Boathouse

The day I saw the message was a Friday.

It started like any other Friday, normal, ordinary, just another precursor to the coming busy weekend.

But that last Friday in August 2021 would turn out to be anything but. It became a tipping point, and a doorway to much change and adventure!

I was lazily scrolling through my Facebook feed, when suddenly I paused at a beautiful picture someone had posted. It was looking out from wooden decking under the clean white canopy of a large gazebo, over a gorgeous loch. There were small boats tethered to a pier wall in the foreground and a cloudless blue sky above brown hills in the far distance.

It caught my eye.

And it caught my heart, as I felt a quickening in my spirit. Deep calling to Deep.

I read the text that came with the picture, and discovered it was posted by Richard, an old friend of mine who had, along with some friends, started a new church a few years prior to the pandemic. They were now meeting in The Boathouse from where the photo had been taken. The post was an invitation to come along.

Have you ever had those moments where it's as if you stop breathing (maybe you actually do?), time seems to stand still, and gravity in that instant releases its grip, you float, everything pauses, and you just stare?
And you ponder.
And wonder.
You're transfixed, and your attention is utterly captured.

Yep. It was one of those.
I wondered what it meant. I think I knew.

And then, just four days later, astonishingly, I received a message from Richard, asking if I'd like to come and lead worship there in that very boathouse, that very Sunday, the 3rd of September.

With God, sometimes there's just no arguing.

He caught my attention with a picture.
Soon He would catch my attention with a people, and a purpose. (Richard's text message to me was quite persuasive too!)

So on that Sunday, I arrived at the Boathouse, guitar in hand, some songs on my mind, some gathered musician friends at my side and some trepidation in my heart, and I met with a new band of journeyers, and wondered, very cautiously, if this might be a thing. If it might be part of the journey through and out and into a bright open space again.

Turned out it *was* a thing.

A lovely thing, in fact.

That first Sunday as a visiting worship minstrel (good phrase!) was followed soon after by other visits, and over the autumn and into the winter, I became a familiar face at the church gatherings.

I got to know new lovely folk who I can now call my dear friends. Very precious. We moved venues sometime later and sadly left the boathouse building behind.

But that was ok, it had served its purpose.
My attention had been caught.

The lovely thing about this time of waking up, was that I quickly felt able to trust people again. I mean, this sounds easy, perhaps trifling.
But it was a huge thing.
Massive.
Colossal.

The folk there built a beautiful bridge of welcome, acceptance and kindness, and I slowly walked over it, wondering if it would hold, and daring to believe it just might.

Don't get me wrong, it was just a beginning.
There was still a whole lot of waking up to go.

A whole lot of self-built protective wall to be eroded and dismantled.
And mending needed to happen.

Lots of mending.

It would (and still will) take time.
Often the unlearning takes way longer than the learning.

But oh, what a beginning!

Thank You, Father.

Thank you for the Boathouse.

From the boathouse looking out onto Loch Leven

7.

The Song

At this point, let me introduce you to Ian. You'll like him.

I've known Ian and his wonderful family for about twenty years. We've done lots of churching together over that time, sometimes we've cried together but also laughed a great deal, he's like a brother.

We've known amazing times with God together, big gatherings with thousands of worshippers and also many small gatherings of a handful, where the gentle moving of the Holy Spirit is equally present and real and beautiful.

Ian plays a djembe drum, and we make a good duo when it comes to worship leading.

I've come to really value his company and his friendship.
With Ian, there are no skeletons in my cupboard.

He knows me.

And to have folk like that in your life is an absolute gift and treasure. I hope you have one or two.

And we do laugh a lot together!

Back in 2004 we had attended CLAN Gathering with our families and friends. It was a fabulous annual Christian teaching and worship week in a big marquee in St Andrews. We'd been before, and we went again.

But in 2004, at the end of the week, a minister called Kenny Borthwick did a talk. It was a call to the church in Scotland to get on the move, to love, to reach out and make a difference. It was very challenging and many of us were very stirred by it.

I came away, and some days later I wrote a song called 'Prayer For The Nation', which embodied something of what Kenny had said. I'm not a prolific song writer, but in this instance, it seemed to beautifully express much of what we had felt following CLAN that year.

One of the lines went,

> 'Lord wake your church that has slumbered too long, awaken the lion, let her roar fill this land...'

The song went into a folder.

And there it stayed, largely dormant.

And some years after that, the great sadness descended and just like the song, I had my own years of dormancy also.

Ian has also had some wilderness years.

And like me, last year there began to be an awakening in his life too. The fact that it happened to us both at the same time was no coincidence. We were meeting up every so often, as friends do, and chatting about where we were with things.

We knew we weren't where we had been.

Nor where we should be.
We weren't hardly even in a place to pray.

We sighed a lot.

We knew something needed to change.
It was good to talk really honestly about that.

It was also good coming out of the pandemic time, to be watching some of the online church services from Martin's Memorial church in Stornoway on the Isle of Lewis.

Tommy MacNeil is the minister there, and Kenny Borthwick from the CLAN days of 2004 was now also involved as a teaching pastor there, so Ian & I had tuned in to some of these services.

And then, in late December, Ian got hold of a book that Tommy had just written.

I remember the day when Ian got it.
He was so excited in a way I'd not seen in a long while!

I met up with him in early January, he'd only just started to read it, and was taking his time with each chapter because it was already causing a tsunami in his soul!

He handed me a copy of the book.

'You must read this!' he insisted as he passed it to me.

I trust Ian, and I believed him.

I took the book from him.

On the cover was the face a lion, strong and proud and regal-looking.

The title:

'Sleeping Giant — a call to the church to awake and arise'

Oh my.

Things were not going to be the same again.

The Lion & the Sleeping Giant

The moment I saw the cover, it happened again – the quickening in my spirit. I was slightly stunned. I knew I was being prodded. I was whisked back to the song I wrote 18 years before. And the lyric about the lion, and a prayer to wake up.

The coincidence became a God-incidence.
Goosebumps became God-bumps.
Father was all over this, and me, and Ian, and the song, and the lion. My heart raced. We were waking up.

On the 11th Jan 2022, I wrote in my journal...

> *'...Ian has given me a copy of the book 'Sleeping Giant', but I've not started it yet. Part of me is too scared. Being a bit lost can be safe and cosy, the easy option. But things are changing. We feel ready to get back in the flow of the river again. Maybe? Yes we do. We feel a stirring which is scary and beautiful and challenging and delightful! The cover of the book reminds me of the song I wrote. I think I should sing that song in Stornoway...'*

And so the song came out of the folder and was dusted off.
And I started reading 'Sleeping Giant'. And like Ian, I was gripped by the call to the church to awake and arise.

The Donut Days

Now, it just so happens that both Ian & I have a penchant for fudge donuts! This is important, as you're about to see.

In Perth there is a Tim Horton's restaurant and drive thru.
They make, undoubtedly and without any questioning, the best maple cream fudge donuts in the entire galaxy. Universe even. Second only to the Fisher & Donaldson bakers in Cupar & St Andrews! (You actually must go and taste for yourself, by the way!)

As we were increasingly stirred by reading each chapter of 'Sleeping Giant', Ian & I decided that we would meet up every 2 weeks to chat and to pray together. We just needed a place somewhere half-way between our distant homes where we could do this. Ahhh, that would be Tim Horton's then. Perfect!

I remember that first time we met to pray like that.

After latte and donutting inside, we went and sat in the carpark in his car.

We began with tentative prayers of thanks:

> *Thank You, Father for the gentle way in which you're waking us up...*

Thank You, Father for the deep patience You have shown us over the past years of sleepy faith, we're so sorry...

Thank You, Lord that you never forgot us or turned away...

Thank You for the fellow travellers we've met of late...

Thank You for the book that has kick-started our faith-engines once more...

Thank You for what the days ahead may hold as we get back in step with You....

Oh, Father....just....thank You.

And so, as winter thawed into spring, the arrival of the warm sun and birdsong, and the budding of hedgerows and fresh new growth around us mirrored something of the process that Father was doing in our lives.

The Waking.

Coming out of the hibernation years was sometimes a bit overwhelming, we had to get over some hurdles that lying for a long time in the sleep-state of faith had created. Our faith-muscles had atrophy.

But it was also a joy.

And we would have moments of no words at all in response to the deep gentle work of Father - the thawing of our hearts, the quickening of our spirits, and the growing realisation that this really was a new season for us.

He was calling us.

He was inviting us to journey closely with Him once again.

Just amazing.

Way better than the donuts!

Way, way better!

10.

The Notion & Many Meetings

It was April 2022. My work singing in care homes and pubs and hotels was picking up massively following two very difficult years of the pandemic live-music shutdown. Ian and I continued to meet. But due to post-pandemic dietary challenges on my part, the donuts stopped. Hey ho.

However, we were being fed something way better.

Our prayers increasingly took on a wider and more national cry, as we prayed not only for ourselves to be properly woken, but at the same time, for the church in Scotland to waken.

One time Ian & I were praying for and talking about Kenny and Tommy way up in Stornoway.

And then came the moment, we had a notion…

> *'Maybe we should go there?'*
>
> The words teetered on the cusp of possibility
> and then landed firmly and with weighty intention.
>
> *'I think we should.'*

In some ways it was a strange notion, but it quickly filled our imaginations and increasingly, much of our conscious chatter too. In tandem, we both felt it was absolutely the right thing to do. There was a seriousness about it.

We had been reading bits of the history of the Hebridean Revival of 1949 to 1953, and it seemed a good thing for us to go to the places we were hearing about, and simply give thanks for what Father had done in the past, and perhaps be stirred to pray for similar awakenings again in Scotland.

We carried on meeting.
Sometimes at Horton's.
Sometimes in a layby somewhere that logistically suited our different journeys that day.

And still the stirring came.
And the praying for Scotland - it got into our wakening DNA.
And faith was rising.
It felt so good to be alive again!

I remember an extraordinary afternoon in May when I was driving back from seeing lovely friends in Manchester. I crossed over the border into Scotland, where the large blue & white saltire sign welcomes those coming home, and I felt an urging to pray out loud for places I passed, for the church in those towns, for Father to awaken others as He was doing with Ian & I.

So I prayed my way up the M74… Gretna, Annan, Dumfries, Ecclefechan (great name!), Lockerbie….. I couldn't seem to stop…Moffat, Abington, Larkhall…it just went on and on… Motherwell, Glasgow, Edinburgh, Cumbernauld… wherever there was a road sign, I prayed for the places named on it… Denny, Stirling, Dunblane, Braco, Muthill, and finally Crieff, where I switched the engine off and sat, croaky voiced, exhausted and drained.

That was an unexpected thing!
It was the waking again.

As Ian & I chatted more about going to the Hebrides, it became clear to us that it wasn't just some road trip, but much more of a pilgrimage. It would be a prayer journey with space and time to reflect, to listen and get to know Father's voice better.

We started to look at a date we could go.
We began to think about wheels, a campervan maybe?
Neither of us had one, nor knew anyone who did.
We asked Father if He would please provide.

Another time, Ian shared with me a picture in his mind that had appeared whilst listening to Father. It was of a barren and dry desert, but where streams of water began to flow and cover the dusty landscape, triggering new life and flourishing greenery as it flowed.

The following week I was at the National Prayer Breakfast in Edinburgh. Lots of dignitaries and MSP's were there, and ordinary folk like me (I did feel rather under-dressed in my jeans and shirt!). As I looked down at the programme I had been given, I saw the bible verse on the front...

'I will make rivers flow on barren heights and springs within the valleys.' Isaiah 41: 17-20

I inwardly gasped. Possibly outwardly too.
Then grinned like a Cheshire Cat and hardly stopped for the next hour. Please Father, do it. Streams in the desert.

Mid July - we met near Perth's North Inch park and sat in Ian's car in the drizzle. We went to Psalm 84. My gaze drifted down to verse five...

> *'Blessed are those whose strength is in you, who have set their hearts on pilgrimage.'*

Wow! Now that was a bit of a lightning strike moment! More grinning. More faith. More expectancy.

We realised we really needed to pin this thing down, so we compared diaries. I rejigged some work bookings and we set the date for September 12th. We would be able to have eight nights away. Really exciting!

And the God-moments just kept on coming.

Firelighters & Beacons

One day Ian was worshipping, and a picture came into his mind of two wee firelighter bricks. They were us. And the bible verse, 'with man this is impossible, but with God, all things are possible.' He was listening to a Brian Doerksen song, 'Light The Fire Again'.

He messaged me to tell me.
More Cheshire Cat grinning.

This was becoming a habit!

Towards the end of July, I met up with a fabulous friend of mine, Lynsey. It was a long-needed catch up. We went for a walk near Loch Leven's Larder (great cakes!) I was telling her about Tommy's Sleeping Giant book and how it had stirred us.

'No Way!' she exclaimed.

With one hand she grabbed my shoulder and with the other, she furiously grappled her phone from her pocket, opened it, and thrust it in front of my face. On the screen was an invitation to a Leaders Day at nearby Lendrick Muir on the 19th August where Tommy would be speaking about the book and what was on his heart for the church in Scotland!

Oh my! God-bumps!

And much excitement!

After a cuppa and a (small) cake, we sat and prayed in my car. We prayed and listened, and Lynsey had a picture come into her mind of beacons being lit all across Scotland, in a chain reaction kind of way.

I told her about Ian's picture of firelighters. More grinning and sharp intakes of breath!

I got home and booked Ian and me some tickets for the Leaders Day with Tommy. (We're not really leaders, but I thought it would be ok!)

Several days later I received a lovely card from Lynsey. On the front was a watercolour painting of a wee VW campervan trundling along a road with tall imposing mountains behind. At the top it said, 'Adventure Awaits', and above that, in biro, she'd added 'A God'. Fabulous! Thank you, LP!

A God adventure awaits! I sent a picture of it to Ian. A grinning emoji face came back!

August – I bought a large map of north-west Scotland and cut out and kept the bit with Harris & Lewis on it, for convenience. We decided to keep the whole journey very flexible and unplanned. But there were a few marker posts that we set in place, things we really wanted to do while there:

a. We wanted to stop and pray in Glencoe on the way there.
b. We wanted to be at the Wednesday evening prayer meeting in Martin's Memorial Church of Scotland in Stornoway.

c. We wanted to be there again on Sunday
d. We wanted to visit Barvas (Barabhais) at some point, where the revival started in 1949, to give thanks.

7th Aug – I was chatting with a church friend, Marc. He said he had a neighbour friend called Derek who had a campervan. Marc would have a word with him about Ian & I borrowing it.

So the days passed very quickly.

Neither Ian nor I could quite believe the pace at which things were happening. Prayers of thankfulness just flowed all the time.

As I drove around the beautiful roads of Perthshire to various gigs, I would find myself praying and praying. My Spotify pilgrimage playlist I'd put together was on all the time.

I was more excited than I had ever expected!

12.

The Bit Where We Get Wheels

Aug 15ᵗʰ - I get a call from Derek. We've never met. We chat for a while, and then, as if reasonably satisfied I'm not a campervan-stealing total road-rage nutcase, he asks do I want to come over and see it?

I message Ian, quick!

We all meet up at Derek's. The van is perfect for our needs. Not too big. Just perfect. He's very happy for us to use it for that week in September!

Thank you, Derek.
And thank You, Father.
Whenever You call, You always provide. Thank You!!!

We sat in Ian's car afterwards. Bowled over. Speechless.
(Spoiler alert - speechlessness would become our trademark response on the journey to come.)

There and then, we booked the return ferry passage from Skye to Harris and back. We had wheels! The ferry was booked!
It was all go!

Can you imagine how we were feeling?

Eight months previously, we were only just starting to wake up. And now all this stuff was happening! And we weren't even on the Great Adventure yet!!!! We were stunned and terrified in equal measure!

Oh My!

Aug 19th - We went to the Leaders Day at Lendrick Muir. Really good to hear Tommy speak about many of the themes in 'Sleeping Giant', and to be with other folk who were clearly on something of a similar journey to us, with a growing desire to see ourselves and the church awake.

At one point I went and chatted with Tommy, and explained about the song I wrote, and how that and the book is partly responsible for us making a journey next month to the Islands. He remembered me from way back when we'd both been at a different leader's day in Perth.

He suggested I sing the song at the prayer gathering on the Wednesday night in Stornoway! Yes please! So that was that!

Grinning, I returned to my seat beside Ian, silently nodded at him and the day continued. So many things were all slotting into place.

Thank you, Father.
Again.

....

So, dear reader, are you ready for a campervan adventure?

Would you like to come with us?

It's gonna be fun!

And you've waited very patiently!

Now might be a good time to go and put the kettle on again, go to the bathroom, and get another slice of cake! (Not that you keep cake in the bathroom.) (That would be weird!)

Are you packed?

Come on then let's go!

13.

The Beginning

Monday 12th September 2022.

My 6am alarm jolts me out of my deep slumber, and I waken. I'm awake. Oh, SO awake!

Like a child who suddenly remembers its Christmas morning, or the day of the school trip, I bounce out of bed to face the day!

Actually, 'bounce' is probably something of an exaggeration. I'm fifty-two. My bouncing out of bed days are well and truly over!

So with as much purpose as I can muster, I creak out of bed! That's better.

I'm packed, I leave the house in the September cool of the after-dawn greyness.

I can smell autumn approaching.
My car journey is quiet and contemplative.

I'm nervous.

8.45am - I'm at the van with Ian and Derek. We load stuff from our cars into the camper, do a final check of everything, say our goodbyes to Derek, and get in.

It's 9.15am. I set my bible open on the dashboard and read from Isaiah 43: 18-21 and 44: 1-5 – the Streams in the desert passages that have inspired and stirred us over the past months.

We both pray.

> *Oh, Father, thank You.*

> *You've brought us amazingly to this point.*

> *This is over to You now.*

> *Please guide and protect and direct.*

> *Have Your way.*

> *You lead us, You know best.*

> *We give you the next 8 days to do what You will, in us and through us.*

> *Amen.*

I close the bible, but not before pulling out the card Lynsey had sent me, the one with the campervan on it and (A God) Adventure Awaits.

I stick it upright on the dashboard.

From here on it would accompany us the whole time as a poignant reminder, that this was all about Him.

And friend, this bit you already know…

I grasp the campervan steering wheel with a white-knuckled nervousness, some apprehension, and much excitement, before glancing over to Ian.

I'm grinning widely, he smiles back.

There's a glint in our eyes, I have butterflies.

I let off the handbrake.
We're on the move!

It's actually happening!

We're going!
Northwards!

14.

Trundling On & Tuning In

Monday.

We had a plan, of sorts.
We needed to be in Uig on the north-east tip of Skye for the 6.20pm ferry crossing to Harris on Tuesday evening, so we drove northwest across Perthshire.

The sun shone intermittently through temporary gaps in grey clouds as we descended the road that closely hugs the steep side of Glen Eagles, with its stunning view across the Strathearn valley to a distant Crieff, my hometown. As we passed through, I wondered how I would feel the next time I saw it, and what new memories I would be carrying with me.

Would I be different? I hoped so.

As we drove, we chatted and pondered and reflected on how we'd got to this point.

We also prayed.

It wasn't the 'let's stop and have a prayer meeting' kind of thing, but instead, our conversations with each other just started to flow seamlessly into conversations with Father. There were three of us in that campervan. It was a beautiful thing to experience.

And it's not left us to this day. I hope it never does.

We would sit in silence too, both content in our own thoughts while feeling the quickening in our spirits to what Father was pointing out, places and people to bring to Him in prayer as we travelled. Sometimes there would be long spells of quiet, and then one of us would just launch into chatting with Father like He was sat there between us. Which He was, by His Spirit, in a profound way.

Often we prayed for places we drove through, for the mending of broken hearts or weary travellers. For church leaders and congregations, for schools and families, for awakenings and stirrings and Father's presence to be known, forgiveness to be experienced, and hope to be found... Just whatever came to mind as we passed through.

I loved that.
I began to realise that that's how prayer should be.
We were tuning in. It was fabulous!
It was like nothing I'd ever known before.

We stopped at the top of Glen Ogle for Ian's 11am coffee.

Now, let me tell you this:
You learn many things about people when you're on a campervan journey with them for eight nights!

I learned that failing to stop for Ian's 11am coffee each morning, no matter where we were, was a grave mistake. He learned that I wake early, I blunder around like a porpoise in a cagoule and spill things, and also that I make a great Thai curry! We both learned lots. And that was also a lovely thing about our adventure.

But best of all, we were learning about Father - His nature, and how to recognise His calming voice above our own sometimes frantic thoughts.

We were learning once again how to chat with Him, respectfully and with reverence and love. But also like you would do with a friend over a coffee & bun in a warm cosy café on a frosty February afternoon. With honesty and laughter, with curiosity and the asking of questions, and sometimes giggling like a child, and often lots of grinning, and sometimes, with the deep exhaling of breath and wonderment.
And at times, something akin to fear.
But not frightening.

It was the waking.

Oh Father Daddy, thank you for being our ever-present companion on the journey.

So we prayed and listened and chatted and pondered our way through Crianlarich, Glen Coe (where we did stop to pray), Fort William, Invergarry, Glenshiel & Kintail, Kyle of Lochalsh, and finally over the magnificent road bridge that straddles the dark waters of the Kyle Akin, and onto the Isle of Skye.

We sang a song as we crossed the high arch of the bridge.

I think you know which one!

15.

The Skye At Night

Driving into Broadford we asked Father for a place for the night to park up. After some to-ing and fro-ing, we ended up a mile or so west of the village on the single-track winding road that leads eventually to Elgol.

As we stopped on a patch of flat sheep-mown grass and turned the engine off, the sun was probably setting somewhere to the west, but we wouldn't have known.

Dark low-lying clouds were falling quickly around the dominating slopes of Beinn na Caillich to the north, and its towering presence stared down at us and our wee home on wheels.

Sighs of relief and some tiredness.

We swivelled the passenger seat round, set up the table, turned the gas bottle on, switched the power from vehicle to leisure batteries, turned the water pump on and switched on some lights - a routine that would become second nature within a day or two.

Suddenly it seemed way darker outside.

I boiled up some pasta twists and reheated a lovely bolognaise I'd made the day before, at home, so far away.

A bottle of wine was opened. We sat and ate and chatted and laughed and wondered about the days ahead. We had expectancy and hope, and a deep peace that Father would lead us well. He is after all, the Good Shepherd.

We prayed our deep thankfulness out to Him, before getting ready to turn in for the night.

At one point, I stood outside for a moment in the total darkness.

There wasn't a sound.
We could have been anywhere.

I shivered slightly.

Partly from the evening chill.

Partly because of the excitement and sense of adventure that was almost tangible.

And partly because of a thankfully fading memory of cold wilderness years that I knew, like my home, were now far behind.

16.

The Requests, the Quiraing, and the Crossing

Tuesday.

We didn't sleep too well. The van was very comfy, but I think our heads were just so full. Months of build-up and preparation and thinking and praying, and here we were, actually on our way! No words! And not much sleep!
That's just how it was.

We had breakfast sitting on a wee bench that Ian discovered just over a rise, a hundred yards from and out of sight of the van. The bench faced west down the glen, to a scattering of distant houses, and had a plaque on it, a message from loved ones to the one who loved the view that we were also now enjoying.

Patches of soft rush dotted the landscape like spiky islands in a smooth green-grassy sea, which sheep meandered between as they grazed. In the morning sunlight, the mountain to our north looked much tamer, but no less stunning.

Now one of the fascinating and beautiful aspects to our whole journey, was that a few folk back home started messaging us prayer requests. We hadn't asked for that, it simply began to happen. And another facet of this was that Father seemed to impress upon us to pray regularly and frequently for a very small handful of those people. Again, this wasn't planned, but we loved that we had time and space to do that.

So that morning, Ian and I sat on the wee bench in the middle of nowhere and spoke to Father and prayed for Lynette from church. For deep healing. And Father's arms to carry her, and the peace of Jesus to settle on her.

We messaged her shortly after on the group chat, and she replied, 'I can definitely say I totally felt God's peace!' And a heart emoji. Thank You, Father.

(A note about phones: Before we left home, we decided that we would keep in touch with folk while we were away. But we turned off all the notification pings, so our journey wouldn't be interrupted all the time. This was a stroke of pilgrimage genius. It meant we only looked at our phones when we chose. Not when they pinged to us. Much better that way round, way fewer distractions. I found that unbelievably refreshing and wondered why I'd not done that years ago. In numerous places, there was no signal at all anyway, and that was actually quite nice too.)

We left Broadford and headed north. I'd not been on Skye since I was a teenager, and my memories of it were fairly sketchy. I was surprised and delighted by how mountainous it was as we passed by Bla Bheinn, Glamaig, and Glen Sligachan on the north-eastern fringe of the Cuillins. Jagged and teeth-like peaks towered over us as we passed by, and fast flowing cataracts tumbled down heathery boulder-strewn slopes. Just beautiful.

We had our music playlists on, and we sang and hummed and worshipped and chatted with Father as we drove.

We felt like we could go anywhere, there was a real freedom. It was amazing!

In Portree we stopped briefly for milk for Ian's coffee, then headed northwards again, up the eastern shoreline of Skye, passing the Old Man of Storr, and reaching the Quiraing at midday.

Now I don't know if you've ever heard of, or seen pictures of the Quiraing, (take a look on Google Images!) but nothing can prepare you for that wildly dramatic and almost prehistoric landscape. We cut left at Brogaig and headed up the sometimes less than single-track road, climbing ever higher, until we reached a series of scarily steep switchback hairpin bends that delivered us up onto the high plateau at the top.

What a view!! We left the van briefly and walked a short way along a gravelly path in the blustery wind, till the vast expanse of the Quiraing and the north-eastern coast of Skye fell away before us in a huge open vista.

I was mesmerised. The massive escarpment to the north was punctuated by impossible rock formations – The Needle, The Table, and the Prison, at the base of which, the emerald green of the wind-flattened grass looked like it had been laid out by a master carpet-fitter. What a place! You MUST go!

Continuing on, we reached Uig at 4.45pm and had time for a bite to eat and drink in the pier café before we rolled into the cavernous belly of the CalMac ferry.

We found a spot up on the open deck to watch the moorings being untethered, and with a great thrumming of engines deep below, and a foamy turmoil of water to the rear, we glided away from the pier, away from Skye, and out into the open sea!

The cloud level was low, a great grey haze hung over the coastline, and gradually Uig was left behind. Harris was hardly visible ahead, and all we had for company were the diving gannets, missile-like and relentless, and far away to the north, the desolate and barren islands of Fladda-Chuain.

I wondered how Saint Columba had felt as he left Ireland and was blown northwards towards Iona, trusting in Father to guide his paths, like us, but so very long ago.

It was starting to get dark as we reached Tarbert at 8pm. We rolled off the ferry and headed down the south road. Our headlamps gave us a narrow and limited view of a barren and dark landscape.

We gave thanks for a calm crossing, and thanks for these beautiful islands that had been the growing focus of our attention for the past winter, spring, and summer.

The darkness fell quickly, and we stopped on a wide flat parking area somewhere above Luskentyre where one other van was already hunkering down for the night.

We were here!

We were in the Hebrides!

17.

When God Came Down

Do you mind if we just pause here for a moment, having just arrived? Take a deep breath because I need to just explain something.

Maybe you're familiar with the stories and accounts of what happened on these islands shortly after the second world war? Maybe not? But it's worth just going back to those dramatic and incredible times.

Much has been written about the Hebridean Revival of 1939, and again from 1949-53. There is a great wee book called 'Floods on Dry Ground' by Jessica Meldrum that both Ian & I had read, it's a thin book, and can be read in a day, but it captures astonishingly something of what occurred. It's worth a read. It's a sobering read too. When God came down and dwelt.

Sometimes we have a cosy and fur-lined idea of what it would be like if only Father's presence and glory was truly seen, and we long for it. But as you read the accounts, something of that changes.

Another much more detailed book we took with us is called 'Sounds From Heaven' by Colin and Mary Peckham. I'll come back to that later. It's an amazing read too!

So back in 1949, in response to a few folk praying persistently and earnestly for months and months, including two elderly sisters, one blind and the other arthritic, there came a moment, in the tiny village of Barvas on the west side of Lewis, where God's presence became tangible, thick in the air.

People were in total fear. They ran from their houses along the lanes to get to the church and other public buildings. They fell on their knees and faces on the roads and cried out for forgiveness and mercy as the absolute holiness of God swept across the fields. They were undone.

There was deep repentance and tears, and the place was shaken, literally on occasions. Daily gatherings for prayer meetings would start at 7pm and would still be going at 3am and longer, spilling over into people's homes, where amazing things continued well into the dawn hours.

Lives were utterly changed. Many people came to faith. There was a love and welcome that permeated amongst people. Church denominations ceased to matter. It was the great awakening, and despite some opposition, it sprung up all over the islands, and lasted on and off for 4 years.

Thankfully we have the written accounts, many from Duncan Campbell, an itinerant minister who was working with the Faith Mission, and he would send weekly reports back to the head office in Edinburgh of all that was going on.

I don't know when he ever slept, he must have been exhausted! It was messy and chaotic. The normality of Church services and programmes was thrown aside.

Here's some snippets of Campbell's reports...

'...Revival fires are spreading and at present it looks like other parts of Lewis are coming under its sway. Meetings have been larger than ever, hundreds have been crowded in, and many turned away. People are bringing their own chairs to sit outside crowded meetings. The meetings continue until 3.00 or 4.00 in the morning... we are dealing with anxious souls in every meeting. I am now at it night and day, and just getting sleep when I can. God is mightily at work. There was a mighty manifestation of the power of God last night. Wave after wave of Holy Ghost power swept over the meetings and strong men were broken down and crying for mercy. Others fainted. People were prostrated on the floor, others with hands raised up fell back in a trance. People walk miles through wind and rain and will wait through three services between 7.30pm and 3.00 in the morning. Men have been found walking the roads at night in distress of soul, other have been found during the day, praying among the rocks...'

I mean. What can you say?
For FOUR years!
It leaves you breathless.
There's never been anything like it in the UK since then.

So as Ian and I turned the light off, that first night on Harris and became cosied up with the sound of the wind and the darkness of the rocky moorland above Luskentyre, with these accounts of the presence and the fear fresh in our minds, we actually felt like we were on sacred and holy ground.

We slept restlessly.

Again.

18

Luskentyre & Leverburgh

Wednesday.

We awoke excitedly to a fabulous view down to Luskentyre beach, and the low green island of Taransay beyond.

After chatting with the lady from the neighbouring campervan (along with her three greyhounds!) (THREE!! In a campervan!!!?), we headed down the tiny dead-end road on the northern side of the bay, parked up and walked down through the dunes amidst swathes of tall marram grass and finally out onto the golden sands.

Once again, I'd seen the pictures, but actually being there...... oh my!

The emerald-green waves rolled continually across the long sweep of sand that stretched southwards around the curve of the high dunes as we ambled along, both lost in our own thoughts and dreams. It was simply beautiful.

The salty wind off the sea filled our senses and the sun shone through gaps in the clouds racing high above. We passed just a handful of people. And some dogs. Where there's a beach, there's always a wee dog or two darting about in something of a frenzy!

My friend Lynsey (who sent us the card) had messaged me, asking for prayer for a particular situation she was facing. I scraped out her initials big in the sand with my feet, and sent a picture of it to her, with the message, 'Praying for you right now on Luskentyre beach. For wisdom, clarity, and a deep sense of 'This is the way, walk in it''. And I sat with my back against the steep dunes and did just that.

Sometimes people need to know you're actually praying for them.

We dragged ourselves away with reluctant hearts, but also with a sense that there was much more to come, and we could always return here if we felt like doing so. We never did, as it turned out. The 'more to come' was better, unbelievably.

Before we left though, I gathered up a small collection of beautiful shells to take home and be a tactile reminder of the short time on Luskentyre beach.

I'm looking at them right now, as I write.
And I will return there one day, to find some more.

We drove southwards along the stunning Harris coastline, past Horgabost and Scarista. The hills on the left swooped down to form a flat grassy plain, the machair, before becoming dune, sandy beach, and finally the foaming sea.

The road wound its way along the machair, passing scatterings of homes, not crowded together, but seemingly dotted about randomly, like a throw of dice. You could see the old boundaries of crofts, and long narrow stretches of vaguely fertile land pointing to the high tide line and where for centuries, generations of islanders had eked out a living here on the edge of the world.

Coming into Leverburgh, I suddenly swerved the van into a carpark in front of an old but recently painted white church building. We quickly jumped out and were immediately struck by a strong notion to pray for this place. So strong was the feeling, that we paced up and down the carpark, stopping to listen, then more pacing.

Goodness knows what people must have thought if they were looking on from the houses dotted around the bay and surrounding hills!

Sometimes you have to just not care.

I opened my Bible, and it turned in the breeze to Isaiah 49 v.20. 'This place is too small for us', I read out, and in the same breath started to pray with urgency that this building would one day soon, become *too small* for all the folk that would want to gather here to meet with Father.

We got back in the van, and Ian picked up the book 'Sounds From Heaven', the revival account by Mary & Colin Peckham. It was like our almanac on the journey and was always close at hand in the van, and as I drove, Ian in the passenger seat would frequently dig it out and read out passages that related to the places we were passing through.

He quickly found the page referring to Leverburgh and read out Duncan Campbell's report from June 1950...

'...I have been up against strong opposition from the usual source, but my eyes are turned towards God and already the

enemy is yielding. My great difficulty is accommodation, as the church is too small for the crowds that are coming...'

Too small for the crowds that are coming.
This place is too small for us....
Ian and I just sat, speechless.

The Holy Spirit hovered around us in the van, I think He was smiling as we tried and failed to find words. So we just slowly shook our heads, and exhaled deeply, again and again. No words, just...oh Father, oh Father. Do it again. Please.

This kind of moment happened repeatedly over the course of the week. 'Thin' moments, where something of heaven glides through and touches Earth.

We weren't at all prepared for it.

How could we be?
We were only just starting to wake up.

It was very humbling and faith-building and left us astounded with no words!

Frequently.

19

Rodel, the Southerly Tip

'*Would you like us to pray for that?*', I asked her gently.

I'm learning that one of the things that begins to happen as you waken from a faith-sleep is that you become more alert to the whispers of the Holy Spirit in you again. Sometimes they are gentle, sometimes a nudge or a wee prod, sometimes a torrent!

On this occasion in Rodel at the southern tip of South Harris, it was the former, but it was a sign we were listening better, and also becoming more confident in chatting God stuff with people. It made me grin.

In Rodel, we left the van and wandered up to the ancient chapel of St Clements. The graveyard was full of very old headstones, nestled amongst more recent ones too. There were other visitors there, talking in hushed tones, as you seem to do in such places.

Having looked inside the chapel, we were making our way back down the well-kempt path that descended in a series of curves to avoid ancient graves and there was a lady standing beside a family tomb.

'Hello, what a special place!', I began.

Sometimes you need to just cast out the fishing line and see if people are interested in chatting. She was.

She started telling us about how she comes to the islands from the mainland because there's a special peace here. I told her we were here on a prayer road trip! We chatted some more.

'I have major anxieties', she went on to explain, 'But when I'm here, they go away.'

Unusually for me, and without too much of a prod I found myself saying, 'It would be great if that peace you feel here would continue with you when you go home. I think Jesus can do that. Would you like us to pray for that?'

'I would really appreciate that, thank you!'

She nodded and smiled and then turned away back up the path, making it clear she didn't expect us to do the praying right there and then. Which was fine. So once back in the van, we prayed for peace for Kirsten, that it would remain with her, and that she would know it was Father. A lovely moment.

And so we continued, looping north, on the very narrow road that hugged the rugged eastern shoreline of Harris, and like a roller-coaster, passed through a succession of hamlets. Many had tiny harbours with stone piers draped in dark low-tide seaweed, that would offer a measure of protection against the winter storms.

It was a foreboding landscape. It was almost lunar.
How they built that road, I'll never know.
Rocky outcrops absolutely covered the undulating low hills. You got the feeling that it was so young, that soil and earth

hadn't really had a chance to form yet. In truth, they are the oldest rocks in the UK. It's just utterly windswept and exposed. Nothing hardly gets a chance to grow.

From one horizon to another there was just great slabs of weathered gneiss, massive metamorphic boulders, grey and pink, shot through with beautiful layers of quartz and darker minerals and spattered with white lichens. In the rare patches between rocks, a trickle of soil and bog offered a variety of heathers and grasses a fragile home.

Somehow, houses had been built amongst this carnage. Remarkable. I'd never seen a landscape like it. We carried on.

We reached the main road and headed through Tarbert once again and on to Lewis.

Harris and Lewis are not in fact separate islands, as there's a narrow low-lying strip of land, just a quarter of a mile long joining the two, upon which the village of Tarbert sits, with a few shops, some homes and businesses, and the ferry pier: it's lifeblood.

We were now heading to Stornoway, a fifty-minute drive northeast, where we would be joining with Tommy & Donna, and the folk at Martin's Memorial Church at 7.30pm. Suddenly it felt like the ambling was over, we were on a main road again, and we had a purpose and a reason! We began to feel a bit nervous, and butterfly-ish again. We were just so excited to be going to the prayer meeting there. Who would've thought!!?

It was a beautiful drive to Stornoway, mountainous to start with, then turning to high moorland and huge wide-open spaces, bleak and empty but for the road and a string of pylons and the odd fresh water lochan.

Ian, ever the fisherman looked on with great interest at each, recounting tales of great trout adventures in his recent past!

On arriving at Laxdale caravan park on a slope overlooking Stornoway, we checked in and found our pitch.

It felt strange to be in the well-manicured and organised setting of a site, rather than in the wilds of nowhere!

But nice too...

There was a lovely toilet block, with showers!!!

20

The Welcome & The Song

That evening, following the last of the pasta bolognaise, we drove down into Stornoway town centre and followed the road as it curved round the north side of the harbour, past the ferry terminal carpark, and to the church building.

I like saying church building. It reminds me that the church is people. Wherever and whatever they meet in.
We don't go TO church, we ARE church.

In our excitement, we had arrived way too early! Tommy had messaged checking we would be there and were still happy to sing 'Prayer for the Nation'. We went inside, there was just a few folk, setting things up. We were warmly welcomed; it was so nice.

There is this thing about being a follower of Jesus, that no matter what church you stumble into, pretty much you're going to make friends quickly. There's a common bond that runs deep. We're all journeyers together. I love that!

I did a quick sound check with my guitar and Ian got his djembe drum in place. More and more folk arrived. Lots of teenagers as well as grown-ups and elderly. And we sat, near the front, as the place filled, looking around, wide eyed and nervous, like two wee schoolboys. It felt surreal to be there, given the terrain we had been in less than a year ago.

So here's the thing. We're not into putting people on pedestals. That's just a folly. We do however have folk in our lives who for years we have trusted and respected and listened to. Tommy & Donna, and Kenny & Morag are such people. And we had been stirred by Father Himself to be here, on this very night, over months of praying and chatting and listening.

And now there we were.
In Stornoway, with them, and a journey and a song.
So I hope you can sense something of the weightiness and sacredness of the whole thing. For some reason, Father God wanted us to be there. That night.
The moment wasn't lost on us. We were shaking!

It began. There was a welcome to the sixty or seventy folk there, a short talk from Tommy, and some worship songs. Then Tommy asked us up to the front and briefly introduced us, and explained how he'd met us back at Lendrick Muir, and about the song I'd written.

I looked out on a sea of lovely faces.
Warm smiles and welcoming expectation beamed back.

Ian began to tell our story of the wilderness years and the discovery of 'Sleeping Giant', and how then we had felt stirred to be praying for Scotland, and as we became more awake, to actually visit here to give thanks and pray.

I picked up on our discovery of the verse in psalm 84 about blessed are those whose hearts are set on pilgrimage, and then how the song, written 18 years ago felt like this was its time, and how we hoped it would be a blessing and a gift to the church.

There was quiet in the room. A waiting.
I found the note and began to sing.

I was quickly lost in the familiar melody and words, and the guitar, and the place and I just worshipped Father as I gave this gift to the folk of Stornoway. Beside me, Ian picked up the rhythm and the beautifully deep resonance of the djembe settled in each corner of the room. I looked on as I sang, amazed to see some folk in tears, and many clearly moved.

The song built and the words filled the room....

Prayer For The Nation

Lord have your way in this land at this time
Let us be light in this nation so dark
Lord change our hearts to beat to the rhythm of praise
Let us go in the strength of Your name

Lord wake Your church that has slumbered too long
Awaken the lion, let her roar fill this land
Restore the full beauty and power of Your bride to be
Let us go in the strength of Your name

Flood this nation O Lord,
Let Your Spirit run free
Giving sight to the blind
Bringing sweet liberty
Let the lame leap for joy,
And the deaf hear Your praise, sing Your praise!
Start with me, start with us,
As we call on Your name.
It is the cry of our hearts,

A prayer for the nation….

Lord we repent of the sins of our land
Facing the cross we submit to your rule
Asking for mercy we plunge into the river of grace
Now we go in the strength of your name.

We finished. There was a silence.
Then quickly a wall of applause erupted.
I didn't quite know what to say, so much was happening, and so I mumbled something largely incoherent about I don't know why you're clapping really, but I hope it was an encouragement. Or some such thing. I've no idea!

I was in an emotional place I don't think I'd ever experienced before. Out of my depth in the sure purposes of Father.

It was precious and wonderful, and I felt a weight had lifted.
The task was done. I'd sung the song in Stornoway, like I had hoped to as I scribbled in my journal way back on the 11th of January at the start of the waking. Never despise the day of small things.

Thank You, Father. You're lovely, faithful, and so, so kind.

But more was yet to come. In the moments that followed.
Unexpectedly way more.

This wasn't over yet.

21.

The Words

Well, I've got to this point in the writing of things, and I'm really at a loss to know how to tell this next bit. Instead of us sitting back down, Tommy asked for some folk to just come up and join us on the platform and gather round Ian & me and pray for us, and if folk felt there was anything specifically from Father for us, to speak that out over us, to bless us.

So, six or seven people surrounded us and began to pray, one at a time. What followed was an overwhelming seventeen minutes of hearing words as if they were coming right from Father.

Beautiful encouragements and words of blessing and affirmation. Words of thanks for what Father had done and was doing. Thankfulness for the song, and our obedience in coming here and singing and praying round the Islands.

There were very specific words too, for both Ian and me, among them, Donna had a picture come to mind of two small firelighter bricks that were starting to ignite. In that instant we remembered that exact same image that Ian had during the 'donut days' way back. We were just trying to stay standing. Tears flowed. Tissues appeared from nowhere. There were other things spoken about where Father was going to lead us next, and about boldness and not being fearful, about old songs gathering dust and new songs yet to be written, about

Father's timing in the waking up, about healing and wisdom, about us both being a bridge over which people would find the love of Christ, about Father making up for the lost years, about the importance of stopping berating ourselves for those years, about weighted blankets being lifted off, on and on it just kept going.

When it did finally come to a quiet end, we just stood there, a mess of tears and emotion.

Only afterwards did we discover to our absolute joy, that both the song and the praying had been recorded and we got sent the link the next day. So grateful, because at the time, we were so bowled over, we just didn't absorb lots of it.

You see, when prophetic gifting (the hearing of Father for the 'now' moment) is encouraged and released in the church, it's astonishing and powerful and faith building and life changing. Truly.

We need more of that in the church, and in the workplace and streets and pubs and our homes, and everywhere.

Thank you, Stornoway church, you wonderful, courageous and loving people!

We sat down, still shaking and clinging to crumpled tissues that contained the tears of our deep thankfulness at what the church had given to us in those sacred moments. It was the absolute blessing of hearing Father's clear voice, spoken as the Holy Spirit moved in ordinary, but bold and faith-filled journeyers. So very precious.

Later, when the gathering drew to a close, there was lots of milling about as the church family chatted and shared stories and caught up on things. Ian and I were again overwhelmed by the response and love from people, many came to thank us.

I showed Donna the pictures I'd drawn in my journal the day Ian told me his fire-lighter picture, which she had just prayed for us too – she was so encouraged!

There was one young man, Duncan, he was tall, with a beaming face and infectious smile as he reminded us that it doesn't matter where we go, God is *so* with us! I loved that!

Thank You Duncan.

Thank you, church.

Thank you, courageous prayer team.

Thank you, Tommy & Donna, Kenny & Morag.

Your welcome and love for two almost-strangers on a prayer road-trip was truly extraordinary.

Every time Ian & I think of that evening, we just shake our heads and exhale.

It was momentous for us.

It really did something deep.
We were changed.

Thank you, dear church in Stornoway.

We left the building at 10.30pm and in something of a stunned and speechless haze, we drove up the road back to the caravan site and settled in for the night.

What an evening it had been!

After lights-out, we lay in the darkness, our thoughts doing a merry dance, our minds full and racing.

We were actually shattered, but once again, even though we really needed it, sleep was elusive, fleeting and unsettled.

We didn't know then, but in the next 24hrs and days following, there was even more to come.

Way more!

Dear reader, you might need another coffee.

Not decaf.

22

Ceann Hulabhaig –
The Undoing & The Mending

Thursday.

When we woke up the next morning, we actually felt refreshed, weirdly. There was definitely a thing happening here. Ian tells me he has always needed a goodly amount of deep sleep otherwise the afternoons are a real struggle. I also love a nap around 4pm, and that wasn't happening either. And yet, with very little deep sleep at nights, we were managing fine during the days.

Amazingly, we discovered a few weeks later that this was a feature of the revival times here too!

Thank you, Father. Strength for the weary.
We were being lifted and sustained.

As we breakfasted (Ian, cornflakes, me, banana and a yogurt) (like you needed to know that?!), we laid the map out on the folding table and leant over it, chatting through a plan, pointing at places and features, contours and beaches excitedly, and wondering what they looked like in real life.

I forgot to say, but a fabulous thing we had discovered the previous night at Martin's Memorial church was that Kenny & Morag would be at Barvas church on Friday night to do an evening service. We knew months ago that we wanted to go to Barvas church building, but we had no notion that there was a Friday evening service this week, that we'd get to go inside, or be at the gathering of the church folk, with Kenny speaking there too, so we were just amazed and stunned about this! It felt like an absolute gift from Father.

Gift upon gift. We grinned all morning!

We prayed and worshipped and sang and poured out our thankfulness for last night, the deep things of God that had been spoken, and the love of people, as well as thanks for the way things were unfolding for the next few days.

Before we left the site, we filled the water tank, emptied the toilet cassette and grey waste, and booked the Saturday and Sunday nights back there too. They had just one space left, amazing!

As we drove out, we were grinning and buzzing! (And we smelled nice because we'd made excellent use of the shower block!) We wondered where today might go!

The plan was to explore and pray round the island of Great Bernera on the western side of Lewis, before looping round Loch Rog, a bit further south and exploring the coast down towards Crowlista and Ardroil, where we'd spend the night parked up somewhere. The following day we'd return northward to Callanish and then Barvas for the evening church gathering.

Rather than the main road, we decided to take the tiny back road out of Stornoway, which ran southwest, becoming part of the Hebridean Way long-distance footpath. It was a lovely drive across the high moorland. The road was empty of traffic as we passed freshly cut and shining peat-stacks and infrequent and isolated stands of wind-blown fir trees. The clouds were high in the sky again, and it was bright with clear visibility for miles.

Around lunch time, we parked up on a short loop of old road which overlooked Loch Ceann Hulabhaig, a beautiful sea-loch surrounded by low hills, rocks, heather, and quietness.

A narrowing grassy promontory extended down into the loch to our left, and in front, a small rocky island poked through the still waters with a collar of brown bladder wrack seaweed.

A lovely spot. I wondered if we might see an otter, or other coastal wildlife.

We had a sandwich and a coffee. And with a gentle breeze faintly whistling round the rim of the skylight, and the smell of the sea in the air, I gazed down the loch and we began to pray.

As is often the case, Father directed our prayers in a particular way, and we found ourselves praying for folk who were carrying disappointments and hurts.

Suddenly Ian stopped, and looked straight at me, remembering something of importance.

'This is the time for Beth's song.' he stated with a calm certainty.

....

Now, I need to introduce you to Beth. You'll love her too.

Beth is a dear friend of ours from way way back. We've done lots of churching together, run youth groups, camps, planted a church, and lead lots of worship together. She has a beautiful voice, and a character to match. Like I do with Ian, I trust Beth. We've gone through lots of ups and downs together, we stand close in the procession of the ragged, we've cried big sad tears and we've laughed uproariously together. We've giggled like children in settings where we shouldn't have, and we've known the powerful presence of Father. She and her lovely family were with us in the CLAN days too. She's hilarious, very creative, and a true friend.

A week before we set off, she messaged Ian & me. She said she would be praying for us, and then there was a link to a song on Spotify.

'I would like you to find a really 'thin place' on your trip, and then play this song at the loudest volume your speakers will allow...' were her instructions. I'd messaged her back, 'I'll not listen to it until we're in that place!'

....

'This is the time for Beth's song'

I retrieved the speaker from its cubby hole, turned it on and connected my phone to it. Scrolling through, I soon found the link in Beth's message, and pressed it.

A song opened up.

It was called 'Your Nature (Live)', by Kari Jobe.
It was 10 minutes long.
I'd not come across it before.
I pressed play.

Now, last night I told you I had trouble describing what happened at the prayer meeting. This is going to be something of a challenge too, more so, as you'll see, but I'll do my best.

As the song began to play, I was leaning back and looking down Ceann Hulabhaig. Something inside me began to well up, I think it was just a deep thankfulness for the kindness and love of Beth that she had thought of us. So kind.

But then as the words broke through the beautiful and haunting opening chords, the welling up turned into a deep eruption of …. I don't have the word. There isn't one.
I began to cry, tears poured down my face in streams.
And I began to sob.
Deep unstoppable relentless sobbing….

> *You bring life to the barren places*
> *Light to the darkest spaces*
> *God, it's Your nature*
> *You bring joy to the broken hearted*
> *Hope to the ones who've lost it*
> *God, it's Your nature*

I cried and cried.

'It's YOUR NATURE'. The phrase cut through to me like a powerful rushing wind. Father doesn't *decide* to be a certain way. He is who He is. He IS love. He IS for me. He IS kindness.

It's His nature. It doesn't change, no matter where or how I'm journeying. Oh my!

My tear-flooded eyes were closed, but memories I'd tried to keep hidden for years in the barren times came into full widescreen focus. It seemed it was time to deal with this.

I felt Father's gaze on me, His utter holiness. He meant business. He didn't want this cloak of sadness on me any longer. His gaze was utterly kind, He felt my hurting too and everything about His face said, 'No more. It's time to stop beating yourself up.' From that moment, I only heard bits and pieces of the song, such was the depth of the encounter, but each time, the words would pierce through the tears and wrap around my heart...

> *There is no desert that Your streams can't run to*
> *There are no ruins that Your love won't make new*
> *You tell the wasteland*
> *That it will bloom again*
> *Cause it's Your nature*

The Holy Spirit was there. Moving and hovering and then settling. This is so hard to describe, but He very gently, but with serious purpose, began to unpeel me.

All the hurting and the disappointment and shame of the wilderness years, and even further back, was laid bare and exposed and I wept for the wasted years and poor choices, and my sin, but then came another lyric....

> *You will restore the years that shame has stolen*
> *You keep the promises that You have spoken*
> *I know this wasteland will be whole again*

Cause it's Your nature

I felt Father's deep resounding love for me. Waves of it.
There was no pointing and wagging of His finger.
No angry face, no judgement at all.
Just the absolute certainty of His holiness coupled with His total love for me.

And it completely broke me.

I was undone. I was a ragged mess, but a cherished ragged mess. There was no hiding, no masks, it was Him and me.

Purity cradling raggedness.

Through quickly drawn breaths I spoke out deep sobs of apology for many things.
I cried and repented and sobbed and my shoulders shook with the overwhelming depth of it all.

I looked up, and across the table Ian was sitting with head bowed and an arm raised, quietly praying. He knew what was happening, and he didn't stop praying throughout the whole thing. At one point he came round and hugged me. I reached up and buried my face in his shoulder, weeping terribly, I apologised to him too, and he just held me, the arms of Jesus, in the flesh. Thank you, my brother.

And then after I don't know how long, through the unending sobs, the Spirit, the Comforter, having opened my heart like a precious book, began to mend me.

Mending me in the very depth of my being where I had stored away all those hurts and failures and disappointments and guilt and shame.

He was the surgeon, purposefully and beautifully, with deep grace and care and precision and love going about His work, healing and reshaping, cutting away deep scar tissue, thawing the cold places, binding up wounds, filling my heart with a steadfast peace like I'd never known. Never.

I could almost hear Him humming away as He worked, like one does when consumed with the important task at hand....

> You bring peace
> To the war inside us
> Speak and all fear is silenced
> God, it's Your nature
> You bring joy to the broken hearted
> Hope to the ones who've lost it
> God, it's Your nature

The song had come to an end a while back, but the lyrics kept washing over me.

> Sing out o barren woman
> Sing out o broken man
> Stretch out your hands believing
>   this is your promise land
> Break out of disappointment
> Break out of hopelessness
> Stretch out your hands believing
>   this is your promise land

I worshipped and worshipped with hands raised high and tears flowing down, and a heart that was full and overwhelmed with the deep, deep work of Father, Son, and Spirit. Three in one.

It was the most beautiful thing that's ever happened to me.

But you know what I'm going to say, don't you?

There was yet more to come, a great gift….

23.

The Motif & The Gift

I don't know how long all that lasted for.
It felt like an age.

My watch actually stopped for thirty minutes during it, then carried on again. We discovered it shortly after and I had to reset it. I don't have a place in my understanding to file that right now. I mean..??

But eventually the tears stopped, and my breathing became almost normal again, and I looked up and smiled at Ian. He took his phone out and found a song and its lovely melody floated through the van. It was a song we'd known for years, called 'Lord I Come To You', and there's a beautiful chorus that goes,

> *'...and as I wait, I'll rise up like the eagle,*
> *and I will soar with You, Your Spirit leads me on,*
> *in the power of Your love...'*

You may know of it.

I smiled, and some tears I thought had subsided leaked out onto my face again. We sang and gazed out down the loch and worshipped and bathed in the moment.

And then to the right, up above the hill at the landward end of Ceann Hulabhaig, I saw a bird lazily wheeling round in slow arcs. In the distance it looked like a buzzard. But as it came closer, I pointed it out to Ian and he grabbed his binoculars.

'It's a golden eagle' he breathed, with hushed excitement

My heart raced.

It came ever nearer.

The wheeling in circles turned into a purposeful glide.

Ian was desperately scrabbling around for his camera, but quickly gave up. We just stared, transfixed!

I was willing it towards us, 'come closer!', hardly daring to imagine it might.

But it did!

It glided slowly towards us, passing just fifteen yards in front of the van. We saw the yellow of its piercing eyes. Its vast wingspan was stunning, and the feathers at the tips of its beautiful wings fluttered in its own breeze.

It passed us and carried on along the shoreline before soaring up into the grey sky and we watched it until it was lost from view, and still we stared.

> Silence in the van.
> A long, stunned, speechless, wide-eyed silence.
> What a gift!

Now, dear reader, there's something you really need to know here.

Sometimes in your journeying, Father will give you what I have come to call a spiritual motif. It can be anything, but the appearance of that thing is a wake-up moment. It's Father clicking his fingers and saying, 'Pay attention here, I don't want you to miss this, it's important, change is happening...'

For me, the motif Father uses, it's the eagle.

From way back, the presence of the eagle, whether it's on a card someone sends, or on a t-shirt I spot someone wearing, or in a song, or poem, or Bible verse, or picture on the side of a lorry, wherever, it's always been a moment to be alert and quickened.

Something is afoot.
Watch.
Be ready.
A change is happening or is coming.
Don't miss this.
It's important.

Sometimes it came before moving house, or a change in job, or another big life moment. My bible cover has an embroidered eagle on it, just in case I should ever forget.

The eagle. It gets my attention.

I knew this full well. And Ian knew this too.
We've talked about it before. His motif is a lion.

And so as that beautiful and majestic golden eagle, king of birds, glided past almost within touching distance, after what had just happened, I felt Father's incredible seal of purpose over the whole thing.

He had got my attention with a song from Beth, and now was sealing that up for always, and telling me that change was here, it was happening now. And it would continue.
A mending and a new start and a changed course.
Remember this moment.
How would I ever forget?

Ceann Hulabhaig.
The mending and the eagle.

Ian & I both shook our heads in that way we were becoming prone to now.

No words.
Deep thankfulness.
Deep worship.

Thank you, Beth, and thank You, Father.
Both of you, for your love for Ian and me.

And we still had Barvas to come.

Oh Barabhais! Oh my!

24.

The Rainbow Sands

There came a point, mid-afternoon, when I felt it would be safe for me to be behind the wheel of a large heavy vehicle moving at varying speeds along narrow and undulating roads again. It took a bit of time, but we pulled back onto the main road just as a beautiful rainbow emerged between the cloud and sunlit hills above the loch. The promise of Father. Always a reminder, no matter where.

From the place of mending & the soaring eagle we drove north and across the new steel girder bridge onto Great Bernera. I'm afraid to say that my journal here does let me down, and my actual memories of being in that place are vague. My head was so full. But I know we did pray at various points, as we had done since we first got in the campervan, aeons ago.

We carried on down the coastline. We had planned to do the loop that would take in Reef, Kneep, and Cliff, before parking up for the night down in Ardoil, but I was exhausted and suggested to Ian that we just go straight to Ardroil where the map suggested there was a huge sandy bay. I was so tired and drained.

But then a beautiful thing happened! As we approached the hamlet of Meavaig, where the loop off the main route began, I felt the tiredness suddenly lift and replaced by a new determination to explore that headland.

And it was just as well that we did!

We turned right at the junction, and right again to begin our circling of the large headland anti-clockwise. It was a beautiful place. Once again, rocky outcrops dotted the low hills and poked through the long grasses and clumps of soft rush.

We pulled up outside a church building again, Uig Parish. And there we prayed with an earnestness that almost matched our Leverburgh experience. Huge numbers of boisterous starlings were gathering along the ridge of the roof and then swooping off the gable end nearest the sea in a wild game of catch-me-if-you-can. It was amazing to watch and hear.

More rainbow moments happened; it was extraordinary. They would appear, briefly but beautifully, then quickly dissolve as the entwining dance of sun and rain flittered on to another place. I think we counted fourteen that afternoon.

Further round the loop, the road descended onto a broad plain of machair, so very different from the rugged and chaotic melee of boulders and crags we had been driving through. It was beautiful. It reminded me of a coastal links golf course. Tiny meadow flowers could be seen, clinging on to the final vestiges of summer, before the gales of winter would turn this idyll into a stretch of barren windswept bleakness.

On the far side, as we passed a caravan site, the road swung upward towards the next hill, and as we gained height, suddenly the most stunning view opened up to our right.

What had been hidden by the low dunes on the seaward fringe of the machair as we drove through it was now visible to us - a long sweep of the most beautiful sandy beach I had ever seen!

In Gaelic it's called Traigh na Beirigh. We called it Kneep beach, as that was the hamlet just a quarter of a mile further on. And we knew with confidence how to pronounce that!

What a place! What a view!

We parked up and wandered down the road a bit and leant on the wire fence beside a gate and just gaped.

The scattering of caravans seemed perilously close to the fringe of dunes that marked the steep edge of the machair.

A stream found its way onto the beautiful silver sands, and as if stretching its arms after the long journey there, it divided into numerous sparkling strands of water that meandered lazily across the end of the bay closest to us. Eventually they spread out in a broad shallow fan before meeting the clear green sea beside a rocky promontory.

On the far side of the beach a low hill rose up, patterned with craggy outcrops. The bay curved away to the left in a huge sweeping arc a mile across, almost encircling the stunning blue-green ocean water, and dotted here and there, miniscule in the vastness of the beach, a handful of people and dogs walked and ran and explored, and, like us, stood and admired.

Across the huge sky, a succession of large white and grey clouds quickly passed over, blown by the prevailing westerly winds, and where there were gaps in between, dazzling curtains of sunshine would suddenly fall on the beach and move across it like a bright golden blanket.

At one point, away on the far side, a sudden rain shower split the sun's rays into a myriad of colours and another beautiful rainbow appeared, rich and bright, arcing across the whole bay and making landfall far along the coastline to the north, what a sight!

I wish you could have been there with Ian and me.

I've not seen a place like that in all my life!

We stood for a while, gazing out over the lush foreground just over the fence where long grasses of all kinds, and dandelion, plantain, cow parsley and purple thistles carpeted the top of the high dune that suddenly fell away steeply to meet the beach down below.

I wanted to run as fast as I could and leap out over the edge!

What a place! Unbelievable!

With huge reluctance, we drove on, and after passing through the scattered hamlets of Kneep and Valtos, the road gained height, and over the next top, we suddenly came upon a wide grassy area, high above the next coastal inlet and houses of Cliff, where wave after wave of Atlantic breakers were sweeping in toward golden sands below us, funnelled in by the high headlands on each side.

We decided this would be our home for the night.
Blustery and dramatic!

Ian and I chatted and prayed a while before lights-out.

We spoke in hushed and sombre tones of all that Father was doing in us.

So very humbling and beautiful.

And serious.

And Joyous.

And Profound.

We never thought the waking would be like this.

We drifted off into to another restless sleep as the van was gently buffeted by the strong Atlantic breeze in the darkness on that high grassy headland, and our dreams were punctuated with images of eagles and rainbows and long curves of sandy coastline stretching away into the far distance.

25

Ardroil and Callanish – Vistas & Prayers

Friday.

The following morning, Friday, after chatting with the two German occupants of another wee campervan that had pulled up shortly after us last night, and giving them directions to Dover (!!), we departed from that high windy bluff, and not long after, found ourselves back at Meavaig, the start of that loop we'd begun yesterday, SO very glad we explored that! Amazing!

We took a right, and the road ran along a deep rocky canyon, vying for space with the clear narrow stream that ran close alongside us.

Coming over a small rise, yet another absolutely stunning panorama announced our arrival at Ardroil.

Framed by lofty mountains behind, a series of vast spotless golden sand bars toyed with the aquamarine waves, stretching wide across the huge bay that was divided beautifully into a series of smaller beaches by long low headlands of grass.

Just beautiful, again!

We couldn't quite believe that these scenes kept coming, one after the other. Astonishing place!

Dear Friend, you MUST go!
(I think I've said that already!)
(And may well again!)

Nestled in at the side of the road amongst some croft buildings and long seized-up and derelict farming machinery, we discovered a fabulous and deceptively large general store which sold everything. Pretty much.

We restocked on some provisions, bought some souvenirs and gifts for those back home. We treated ourselves to some smoked trout and oatcakes, and due to the very helpful local lady at the till, I learned how to properly pronounce Ceann Hulabhaig!

Kee-own (rhymes with brown) Hula-vegg.
I expected to have to retell that part of the adventure a few times in the months ahead and wanted to get it right!

We backtracked just up the hill and parked near the school, pointing the van southwards to face the wide-open view.

Once again, the sun was shining through bright blue gaps between fast moving white fluffy clouds, resulting in the same view changing again and again from moment to moment as the light and shadow, brightness and contrast ebbed and flowed continually.

It was quite mesmerising.

Ian made his café latte, and I tried to journal something of the past 24 hours. My writing was a mess, reflecting something of the state of parts of my head, truth be told.

Still, we sat and gazed across the bay of Ardroil with brief bits of chat and prayers of thanks and amazement while drinking in the view.

We had a song playing, which was virtually on repeat over these days, called 'Creation Calls', by Brian Doerksen. Have a listen to it now on YouTube or Spotify! It beautifully captures how we felt as we looked out over these west coast beaches and landscapes.

> *'How can I say there is no God, when all*
> *around creation calls...*
> *A singing bird, a mighty tree, the vast*
> *expanse of open sea...*
> *I love to stand at ocean's shore, and feel*
> *the thundering breakers roar...'*

The lyrics became part of that vast landscape before us and we hummed and sang and worshipped along.

Precious times and moments.
We didn't want to leave.

There were some places on our grand adventure that we knew one day we will return to. Kneep and Ardroil were two of them, for sure.

Oh, and dear Barvas!

We drove back, retracing our steps of the past two days, and as we passed by Ceann Hulabhaig I glanced upward to see if by chance or design, our eagle was still floating about. It wasn't. But that was ok. I don't know if I could've coped with another sighting! We drove on, heading to Callanish.

Everyone who visits Lewis goes to Callanish, apparently. The standing stones there possibly pre-date Stonehenge and were placed around 5000 years ago. It is a magnet for those interested in bronze age neolithic monuments and sites.

It's also got a lovely wee visitor centre with a café, toilets, shop and museum! Which was nice!

We left the van in the carpark and walked up to the stones. It's undoubtedly a special place, and photos never do these locations justice. To touch these upright megaliths is to touch the deep past and brush hands with folk who were probably really similar to us, with the same concerns, anxieties, hopes and dreams and desire to connect with the otherness of the One who made it all. Very similar.

Except they didn't have campervans.
But they did have a desire to travel great distances, which the evidence suggests they did, by way of the seas.

As we got back in the van, we checked messages. There were urgent and serious situations that we knew we needed to totally focus our prayer on. So we called out with reverence and persistence to Father, and named those back home who needed His healing touch right now. Neil, our percussionist at church, now in hospital with a very serious eye infection. Lynette, and Beth. Fellow journeyers feeling the deep pains of living in a very broken world.

So we prayed, as Jesus taught his friends one day on a hillside in Roman-occupied Palestine...Your Kingdom Come, Your will be done on Earth as it is in Heaven...

And in that ancient place of Callanish, where we and a distant people group are separated by a vast tract of time, we prayed for Father to slice through the distance that separates Heaven and earth and touch our time and space right now. For our friends and those weary on the journey.

Do it, Lord, please...

Moments after we had prayed, we messaged, and a reply came from Lynette, 'Thank you!' and a wee note to say how she had felt growing despair today, and now not.

Thank You, Lord.
Your timing is, as always, perfect.

We drove north.

Next stop, Barvas.

26

Barvas, O Barabhais!

Like so many of the villages we had passed through since arriving on Lewis, Barvas was a very loosely arranged scattering of houses. There were modern bungalows set between much older dwellings that had stood the test not only of time, but the annual ravages of the North Atlantic storms that batter this first bastion of civilisation after their long journey from the Americas, Canada and Newfoundland.

Barvas sits in a dell, with long shallow slopes that rise gently to the south and north. The land is not the best quality. There are Highland sheep and livestock dotted about, but you get the impression that life is still hard here.

On Lewis, survival is not something you go on a Bear Grylls course to learn about. For generations it has shaped the people and their actual way of life here on this beautiful, barren and constantly wind-blown land.

The pace of life here is vastly different from mainland life too. Everything is slower, wonderfully so, from the traffic on the roads to the expectations of deliveries, and this is beautifully reflected in the way the Islanders talk.

Conversations are gentle, thoughtful, and regular pauses, way longer than you'd normally feel comfortable with, are a lovely feature of gently flowing dialogue. We loved it!

Just being with the local folk made you relax and breathe and stop and ponder. It's part of the allure. We were to experience this first-hand with the wonderful Barvas church family in the hours to come.

After arriving and parking up the van in the large, deserted carpark that formed a U-shape around three sides of the white church building, we got out and went and stood on the pale grey steps that led up to the double front door.
There was no-one around.

So much of what we had read in the past months about the Great Awakening revival here was suddenly vivid and fresh again in our minds. We were standing on the very steps that folk had queued on for hours day and night to get inside this packed-to-overflowing church building, as God's powerful presence and utter holiness caused chaos all around.

We looked out over the empty main road and across the machair to the sea and wondered what on earth it must have been like. And whether we knew what on earth we were doing by praying for God to visit again??

A cold wind was blowing in off the rugged shoreline where we could see blasts of spray erupting into the air as persistent waves attacked the dark rocks in a relentless onslaught of foaming breakers.

In that cold windy moment, Ian was on a prayer-wander and disappeared around the side of the building for a moment. I sat down on those feet-worn steps, heavy with the legacy of seventy years, and prayed.

A verse from the prophet Habakkuk came to mind and I battled with the breeze to find the place in my bible. Ch 3 verse 1….

> *'Lord I have heard of Your fame, I stand in awe of Your deeds, O Lord. Renew them in our day, in our time make them known; in wrath remember mercy.'*

What else does one pray, in the very place where a great outpouring of Father's power, presence and holiness had blanketed the air and for a time turned the world upside down?

So, with a genuine measure of fear and sombreness, I prayed those ancient words again, and the wind whisked them from my lips and away out over the barren fields…

Renew them in our Day,
Father, please….in our time,
make them known….

27.

The Bit Where We're Overwhelmed, Again

We sat back in the van for a while. The outside cold was more than we were dressed for, so we waited quietly in the relative warmth and chatted and prayed some more. As always, much thankfulness for the journey that over years and months had brought us both very unexpectedly to this moment.

It was Friday evening, the 16th of September.

This weekend was Communion weekend for the church here, and it's much more of a thing than in many churches elsewhere. They have a Friday night gathering, another on Saturday night, the Sunday morning communion service, and finally a Sunday night service of Thanks. It's a great idea actually, a really beautiful way to approach a special time in the life of the church family together.

So Ian and I sat with that same mixture of expectancy and nerves that had come over us on Wednesday night in Stornoway.

A few folk arrived in the carpark and went down the far side to a door into the back hall. We jumped out and followed them once they were in, knocking on that same door, and wondering how on earth we would even begin to explain who or what or why these two strangers were here!

The door was opened, and we said a rather faltering hello, introduced ourselves and before we could really explain ourselves, there was a cheery 'Oh! Come away in!', and we were warmly ushered into a lovely warm carpeted room. Hands were shaken, some explanation made of our journey, and the smiling faces of these fabulous people dissolved away a goodly layer of our nervousness.

They were genuinely delighted we were there! Some ladies were arranging a spectacular array of cakes, scones and pancakes for later – this was my kind of church!!

We felt terribly under-dressed, wearing jeans and casual shirts, while all the folk arriving were in smart clothes, but the thing was, we never ever felt that it was an issue for anyone at all, and if there was any discomfort in it, it was all self-imposed on our part, and even that quickly evaporated in the warmth of the welcome and kindness we were experiencing.

Kenny & Morag from Stornoway church appeared, so lovely to see them again! As they were going through into the main church bit via an adjoining door from the back hall, Morag paused, looked at Ian & me, and said, 'You two are going to be heralds to the nation.' There was no time for any further explanation as she & Kenny had to continue through the doorway, and she disappeared.

!!??????? What do you do with a moment like that?????!!

We actually just slumped down in unison into two nearby chairs, and stared at one another and shook our heads, stunned, speechless.

The thing about a prophetic word, is that it often carries immediate weightiness in your spirit, and we both felt it, but neither of us had any clue what it meant in that moment, or quite where to store it, so all we could do was gape! That sensation of being overwhelmed by events totally outside our imaginings and control was again rising within us.

Since that day, in chatting about that moment, Morag has explained that she hopes Father will use us in music and testimony to awaken others, like heralds with long and far-reaching trumpets.

Thank you, Morag - it's such a lovely thing to hold on to, and we pray that somehow it will come to pass in the days and months ahead.

But at the time, as we sat there in the back hall of Barvas church, we just focussed mainly on breathing and looking like everything was normal!

28

The ALL of Me to the ALL of Him

Shortly after, everyone in that back room gathering space was ushered through into the main church and we all found seats, and once again, Ian & I wondered what it must have been like to be in this very building, seventy-odd years ago.

I have a great photo that I quickly took on my phone as I checked to make sure it was on silent. The photo is of Ian beside me, hands over his mouth in a sort of awe-stricken moment of utter bewilderment at where we were and what was unfolding, I love that picture!

The service was led by the minister, Dougie, a lovely guy from the north of England (the story of how he ended up in Barvas was amazing!) and during it there was the singing of psalms, beautiful and unaccompanied, just our voices filling that sacred space.

Kenny preached, and oh my, it was the kind of talk you could listen to over and over. Kenny has a wonderful gentleness about how he speaks. He doesn't rush things at you. There's space in amongst each precious gem of truth or illustration or beautiful anecdote or scripture for you to reflect and absorb.

And absorb we did!

As a precursor to the communion service on Sunday, he talked about the pilgrims of old who would make the perilous journeys to Jerusalem to meet with others and encounter God during the great festivals of worship, as described in psalm 121 and others following.

Ian nudged me gently with his elbow. We didn't need to make eye contact. We both knew. Pilgrims. I had goosebumps again.

The message was a call, a plea to approach Father not hiding stuff away, or leaving our issues and baggage at the door, but bringing the whole of me to the whole of Him, the All of Me to the ALL of Him.

That's worship.
Coming to Him just as we are.
It's the only way.

It was a stunning message, simple yet profound, and wonderfully delivered.

He closed by saying, '…so here we are… pilgrims…'
And we felt Father's presence in that place, I think everyone there did. It was beautiful.

The talk is posted on the Barvas Church Of Scotland Facebook page, Sept 16th 9am, and on their Spotify page. I do hope it stays there a long time.

I wish everyone in the world could hear it and understand how we approach Father, with all of me, my sin, my vulnerability, honest and ragged, and we give that to the ALL of Him, who welcomes every time, again and again, with strong open arms, and deep, deep love.

....

Following that part of the service we all trundled through to the back room again, where, after collecting a coffee from the hatch through to the wee kitchen, and loading up our plates with some delicious sweet things at the long table against the rear wall, we all sat around in small groups and chatted.

It was great just being there with these lovely folk, hearing their stories, and sharing some of ours. It was remarkable how quickly we felt totally welcomed and part of all that was going on. We laughed and chatted and listened and treasured this family time with Josie & Sammy & Lorraine, Angus, D.I, Dougie & Joan, Donald and Chris-Ann, Ian, and cheery Colin, just some of the names we got to know.

And then as Dougie walked past, he suddenly said, 'I hear you've got a song, would you like to sing it for us?' I never did find out, but I do believe Morag was responsible for that!

Having no words and being wide-eyed is fine when it's just Ian and me in the van, it happened loads and we were getting almost used to it.

But when it happens in public, after being asked a very normal question and people are listening in, it's kind of awkward!

We managed to convey a yes somehow, and we quickly crept outside into the cold and darkening evening to get the guitar and djembe from the van. We stood there in the dim light at the rear door storage compartment for a moment, trying to comprehend many things, and breathe..!

- We were in Barvas village.
- We were at the church.
- We had been able to come inside.
- There was an evening service.
- Kenny and Morag were there.
- Kenny was preaching.
- We'd met the loveliest of people.
- And now we had been asked to sing the song, 'Prayer For The Nation' again!

Almost exactly nine months ago I had hoped we might sing it one day in Stornoway. Which we had. And now, we were about to again, this time in Barvas - holy ground if ever there was.

Father, you are astonishing. Truly.

Thank You so very much.

We went back inside, and everyone was going back into the main church for a shorter time of sharing and some songs. Someone picked the song 'Take My Life And Let It Be'. It's an old hymn, and amazingly it had been the song we sang as I was baptised as an eighteen-year-old in Helensburgh.

As I went down into the baptismal pool on that evening in 1988, we sang the third verse, 'Take my voice and let me sing, always, only for My King…' Little did I know at the time of how prophetic that was.

But as Dougie introduced Ian & me, and we stood on the platform, thirty-four years later, guitar in hand, the significance of that verse, that hymn, and where we now stood was not lost on me, and I smiled, and silently whispered to Father,

'You Knew! All along! Thank you!'

So we sang. And once again looked out over faces of people who, two hours ago we'd never met and who hadn't a clue who we were, but whom we could now count as our friends.

Such a beautiful thing!

As before, the song built, and the rhythm resonated around the walls of that building that has witnessed many extraordinary moves of God, and lives changed, and hope found in Jesus. What a privilege.

Oh, Barvas!

Thank you so much for your beautiful welcome.

....

Dougie said it would be fine for us to sleep in the church carpark that night.

So we did.

29

Sleeping On Holy Ground

I would love to be able to tell you that it was a really deep and restful sleep at last.

But, again, no.

As was now the norm after lights out, we lay awake in the darkness of the van for a long while before sleep found us.

There were so many thoughts that were flitting around in our heads, like a kaleidoscope of swallowtail butterflies on a summer's day, searching endlessly along a green hedgerow for the right branches on which to finally settle.

We quietly chatted for a short while, but both of us quickly got overtaken with our own silent reflections on the way the past few days had unfolded. There was so much to take in and sift through and try and process.

So we lay in that silence, listening to the gentle whisper of the wind on the seaward side of the van and thinking back to what we'd read of the revivals of yesteryear.

We were lying there, in the very spot where it had all begun.

It was quite something.

And even though it was against the pillow, I think I probably shook my head a number of times in ongoing amazement.

As I snuggled my duvet around me, cocoon-like in the near-total darkness, I remember saying quiet prayers of thanks under my breath and marvelling at the adventure that we were walking in.

I also felt something of Psalm 121's description of Father's continual care and watching over us, in the waking and the sleeping.

And then the welcome sleep finally came to us...

...Just a few paces from the grey steps of Barvas church.

A very special day.

Interceding, Ness,
and the Goodness of God

Saturday.

I awoke early and leaning up on one elbow, I quietly lifted the bottom fringe of the curtain beside my head and peered outside. Across the rough brown moorland to the east, the sun had not long risen and the orangey morning dawn colours that painted the gathering clouds were beautiful.

The patch of cold window in front of my face quickly misted up under the warmth of my breath and I lay back down again, wondering what today might hold.

'Good morning, Father', I whispered.
And another day in His close company began.

It was 7.30am. Ian was still sleeping.

I quietly opened my phone and messaged Beth to send some pictures, but mainly to say thank you again for the song she had sent us which Father had so beautifully used to trigger some deep mending in me at Ceann Hulabhaig.

It turned out she was also awake, and with little delay her reply came back:

'That was simply the best message to wake up to! Wondering if you could pray for me this morning, I am in the pits of shame and despair, I keep falling when I'm complacent...pray that I would fall up, not down.'

Some more messages went back and forth, and then I sent this...

> Oh Beth, absolutely of course we'll pray. We will start the day with this shortly. We love you. Father loves you. There is no shame we're meant to carry. We will hold you in prayer all day and following. I still carry the shame and deep disappointment in myself at failures in my marriage breakdown, etc, and so many other things too, but Father says NO MORE. He mends the broken hearted, that's his nature.
> Swim in the open river of that, Beth.
> Bring your All of You to the All of Him. That's what worship is. He understands and deeply feels your pain. He knows we won't be perfect till on that Day. So there's no shame to be carried. The cross is totally sufficient, overwhelmingly so.
> He loves you Beth, and He's very proud of who you're becoming and how you're still following hard after Him despite and through all the blips and failure moments.
> Don't despair. He will lift you, 'and as you wait, you'll rise up like the eagle..'
> Love x

I stood up to put the kettle on, and Ian was just stirring, so I told him of Beth's message, and through the gentle background hiss of the gas stove, we prayed right there and then for her. Ian had the word 'Overcomer' settle in his mind, and we prayed that word for our dear struggling friend so far away and then messaged that word to her with an explanation soon after.

Coffee, and another message came in, Neil in hospital with his eye infection, there was a real danger that his eye would need to be removed unless things changed quickly, his cornea was only one or two cells thick in places. We cried out to Father again and again, Lord, in your mercy, please change things, please heal, please protect, please intervene, complete healing…Your Kingdome Come!

Moments later a message from Lynette, she'd posted on the church worship group chat, 'I'm so struggling, my voice has gone, throat awful, my eye is infected…' Her immune system disorder means that she lives every day with the worry of getting any infection that is then totally debilitating. So we prayed on even while getting dressed, we didn't stop. It was a time for interceding, standing in the gap and pressing into Father for deep change in fragile lives far away.

And this was the privilege and the pain.

We had the space and time to devote to calling out to Father on behalf of our dear friends back home, and our hearts went out to them in their trials, but part of us wished we could be there and hug them right then. We couldn't. But Father could and did.

This is church, carrying one another in the procession of the ragged, but beautiful in Jesus' eyes, and His bride-to-be.

And then my son Callum from Buckinghamshire phoned me. He was asking for us to pray for him regarding some big life choices that he was feeling were about to come, and he didn't know quite which way was best. So we prayed on...

It was almost eleven o'clock when we finally left the church carpark in Barvas, and headed north again, up to the very tip of Lewis, a wee place called Ness. The landscape as we drove north was unforgiving, desolate. There's no doubt a wild beauty to it, in its own way, but the softly undulating slopes and peat-cut swathes of brown heather stretching away to the east felt somehow very forlorn.

The long straight road took us through the wee coastal settlements of Borve, Galson and Dell. At one point we got a strong feeling to pray for Ian's wife and three daughters, which we obediently did. Sometimes you just need to act on those feelings without delay or question.

The Butt of Lewis is the island's most northerly point. Sailing north from this point, you would arrive next at the Faroe Islands, 250 miles of cold ocean later. And after that, the Polar Arctic. There was something quite fascinating about standing at the absolute extremity of land and gazing out at seemingly endless sea on three sides.

We parked only for a short time there and in the shadow of the red-bricked Ness Lighthouse, we stood on the very edge of the high cliffs and stared fixatedly at the huge ocean swell below as it tore into jagged towering columns of black spray-drenched rocks. The power of the waves was immense, dramatic and unceasing.

Grey seals bobbed in the white water, and gannets, shags, skuas and gulls dotted the chaotic pinnacles of broken cliff, diving and shrieking at the foaming tumult. The cold sea-wind blustered across our faces, turning our cheeks rosy, as a frosty winter's day might.

As we began the return journey, we had a proper stop just south of the lighthouse where a beautiful narrow sheltered cove channelled slow green waves up onto a steeply sloping golden beach. We had a (late) coffee, and some (early) lunch, after which I stumbled down an uneven path onto the sparkling sands for short time.

It was lovely to be out of the wind, and just watch wave after wave rolling in, while trying to judge the exact maximum reach of each wave and stand right there, defiant! And wet footed, as it turned out! My judgement was poor!

We headed south again. At one point we pulled into the carpark of what may have been a campervan site, or a training centre, or council run offices, it was hard to tell. But we started to pray again for Beth, Lynnette, Neil and Callum. Sometimes you just run out of actual words, and in those moments, there's just a deep calling to deep where the thoughts in the silence are enough and are heard.

I checked messages. There was an email from Tommy in Stornoway. Would we like to sing 'Prayer For The Nation', and also another song I'd penned called 'Sing To The King, Sing Praises' at the Sunday evening church gathering?

We grinned. And I quickly sent the reply, 'Yes, please, we'd love to! Thank you!'

This was the 'More' of God.

The thing is, we often feel like we don't deserve much from Father, or that it'll always be just the economy package or cheap option or just the very least. But in contrast, we were realising that Father has much in store for us, always, and when we take the time to really connect with Him, things happen that go way beyond what we had hoped or imagined. It's His nature to bless and give us all good things in Christ.

I wish we believed that a bit more in the Church today.

As we drove all the way back to Stornoway, we chatted about the need to keep the 'me' out of the way each day. Less of me and more of you, Lord. Forgive me for my ego and pride. Quell them, keep them in check, and let my life be always pointing to You, Father, so You get all the glory in all things.

We were serious. Humility, it's a daily battle that if lost, can wreck what Father is trying to do in and through us.

So we were thankful for all the gifts upon gifts that we were experiencing and we prayed so to the great Giver as we drove south then west, and tried not to doubt His kindness and goodness and love.

But as if to really drive home the point to us...

We reached Laxdale caravan site on the western edge of Stornoway, and I went to check in at reception. Standing behind the desk was a lady we'd not seen on the Wednesday when we were last here.

She said 'hello' and asked if we were having a good trip, touristy questions and the like. Her name was Diane. I said, 'Oh yes, and we were in Barvas church last night, and we sang!'

Without missing a beat, she exclaimed,

> 'Oh! You're THOSE guys!!'

And without missing the next beat either, she closed the reception bookings diary and said,

> 'This one's on us!'

I must have looked puzzled, appropriately so, because I was.

> 'This one's on us, no need to pay.'

Turns out, she and her husband Gordon own the caravan site. They're both Christians too. Gordon was at Barvas and heard us sing last night, and now Diane, as a 'thank you' for what we had done and were doing on the Islands, was standing in front of me, telling me that they would pay for our time here.

Sometimes we're a bit thick in getting the message from Father. So sometimes He makes it unequivocally plain, and blindingly obvious that He is FOR US. And when you glimpse it for real, and see and taste and experience it, it makes you shed a tear.

Why is that?

Maybe, because very deep in the hurting places, it's so very hard to believe it's actually true. Our culture teaches us we have to earn and pay for anything good.

But Father IS good, it's His NATURE.

When, Oh when will we learn?

I crossed the gravel back to our pitch and told Ian.
We smiled at each other while both shaking our heads and he said, 'Oh Father, thank you!'

We were really tired on that Saturday evening, but as we tucked into the venison & plum chutney pies that Ian had brought from home and which had been in the bottom of the tiny fridge all this time, we suddenly realised that if we were going to Martin's Memorial to sing tomorrow night, it meant that we could now go back to Barvas tomorrow morning to be with the church family there again for the Communion service!

Big smiles!

Gift upon gift.

Kindness upon kindness.

I think our continual grinning and shaking of our tired heads and deep exhales of amazement were understood by Father as our thankful worship.

I really do hope so.

Because words were increasingly failing us.

The Silent Road

Sunday 18th September

The next morning, we drove back to Barvas in silence.

The long straight road across the island looked like it had been just rolled out over the brown peat-cut landscape as one would unroll a carpet. The trident-shaped electricity polls, some at peculiar storm-blown angles, ran in parallel to the empty road, passing a very occasional lonely square of pine trees. The sky was an uninterrupted ceiling of misty grey, but the cloud level was high and there was, unusually, little wind.

There was a calmness.

And the quietness was a soothing balm.

Like I said, we didn't talk.
I wasn't even sure what could be said, really.

Our hearts were contented, and our minds were full as we covered the twelve miles, and our voices were stilled by the overwhelming sense of all that Father was doing in us and through us.

Returning to Barvas!

It seemed surreal, but so very welcome.

We arrived way too early for the church service, such was our excitement to be back there, and we parked up in the same spot as before and turned the engine off and sat quietly.

We had an hour to wait.
It made us smile.

And then, something rather unusual and surprising happened.

Which led to a further profound thing happening.

And that profound thing in turn caused another unplanned and unexpectedly worshipful moment!

And the following day we would again be reminded of this moment with stunned amazement!

Read on.......

32.

Don't Pray Now!

So we were sitting in the van, in the carpark of Barvas church. I was about to launch into praying for Beth, Neil, Lynette and others, when, before I even had a chance to, very clearly and suddenly, Father's voice spoke into my thoughts...

> *'Wait. This time is between you and I now.*
>
> *Don't be in prayer for them in this moment.*
>
> *I've got them. They're covered.*
>
> *Just you two, and Me now.'*

Oh my...

I had some moments of confusedly blinking and wondering if I'd heard right. It seemed an unusual thing for Father to say.

So I shared it with Ian.
It sat right with him, and he nodded quietly.

And so we just sat and did what we'd been told.

....

And in quietness, simply brought the All of Us to the ALL of Him.

....

Quietly, we whispered our worship.

....

On hallowed ground we praised His hallowed Name.

....

Everything in us was still, and fully focussed on Father God.

....

And we waited on Him. No rush. No agenda. Just waiting.

....

And we listened, eyes and ears and minds open to what He might say next.....

...It turned out, it was about cows!

33

The Cattle and the Promise

I love the myriad of ways in which Father speaks to us all, you and I both.

His written word, the bible is crucial and fundamental in our learning of who He is. But as I heard someone once say, He didn't write a book, and then lose His voice.

He calls to us through creation, the beauty round about us that sometimes makes us gasp and sigh and shake our heads in wonderment.

And He speaks right into our thoughts. Often.

You may not realise it all the time.

I think a lot of the time we don't recognise His voice for what it is. I think often we're so caught up in busyness that the 'still small voice' is lost to us.

Or perhaps we don't realise that the sleeping dreams or waking ideas and thoughts that we have are sometimes from Him, sown gently into our minds as a call to seek Him, and find Him.

But I do love His creativity in how He gets our attention, and how He uses all our life experience and knowledge and interests and passions as a bridge over which to walk and share His heart with us.

And that is exactly what happened next.

Ian was looking out of the window, across to the far side of the main road where something had gotten his attention.

Behind a weary and tottering fence sat an old yellow item of farm machinery, nestled against the remains of drystone shielings. Beyond that, in I suppose what you'd possibly call a field, but with none of the usual characteristics, there were a handful of cows.

Ian turned to me and spoke with a clarity and conviction.

He explained, 'Those hardy cattle there, they are sought after and bought up by farmers from the central belt of Scotland. The reason is they have harder and rougher pasture here, and their growth rate is much slower. But when they are placed in the fertile and lush pasture much further south, they very quickly grow, way quicker than normal, and strengthen and flourish.' Ian grew up in the farming community. He knows these things.

There was a pause, and Ian continued...

'Father is saying to us, 'You've been in barren places, but now I'm moving you to a new place in life, a season where you will flourish and grow way more quickly than you'd expect.' From barrenness to a place of flourishing.'

Oh my.

Once more, the weightiness of the word quickly fell upon us both, and I felt a welling up inside me. Another undoing moment. The tears that quickly began to flow again were tears of deep gratitude, flowing from a deeply humbled heart.

And as I felt Father's total loving commitment to us and absorbed the word of His promise of moving us from barrenness to undeserved flourishing, through more tears and a runny nose I found myself confessing my poor choices of the past few years, and I brought them to Father.

And then Ian joined me in prayers of deep worship to the One who had patiently rescued us and brought us through and breathed new life into our bruised and weary spirits, and then brought us here, to Barvas, where so many folks have been undone and known the promises of Father, and set on a new course, too.

From a place of barrenness to a place of flourishing.
Here He was doing it again, in us.

'Oh, Father, Daddy…

'Thank you' is such a poor word to try and express what we actually feel right now.

It was a fitting way to approach Communion.

34.

The Bread and the Wine

I put my hanky away as folk once again began to arrive and park up. Cheery Colin (he doesn't know we call him that) was one of the first, we jumped out of the van and went over to chat. What a lovely man, we felt he had many a story to tell!

He made us smile and laugh.

Others arrived, and we joined them. As we climbed up those now-familiar grey steps to the main front door, I felt that I should remove my boots, and enter the building in socks, 'for the place you are standing on is holy ground.' Now I don't know if that was the Spirit or just my own feeling, but it sat right with me either way, and I spent the next ninety minutes unshod.

We sat 3 or 4 rows back in the middle on the comfy blue cushioned chairs. Thankfully, gone were the days of hard unyielding wooden pews!

Once again, the welcome from the church family as they gathered was beautiful. Lots of people who we'd met on Friday night came over and said Hi with beaming faces. Josie, Sammy and Lorraine came and sat to my left, that was nice. I felt a connection with them that I couldn't really explain, so I was glad they were there.

Kenny & Morag appeared, and we nodded and smiled our hello as they passed. I silently prayed for them both. Kenny has a chronic respiratory condition that is being managed but it means he gets very tired quickly. He almost died some years ago before the cause was discovered – mould in the church manse – and since then has recovered significantly, but it's still difficult. He nearly gave up preaching and teaching altogether, but so thankfully he didn't, he's very gifted and a real inspiration to many. I prayed that Father would give him energy and the words for both services today, and for many more to come.

At one point I leaned forward and spoke to Lorraine. During the cake chats on Friday night, with curiosity I'd asked her how she best connects with Father and she'd told me that she goes running along the machair and meets with Him there as she prays and runs. I asked if she'd run yesterday, and she said no, she had a sinus problem but it's no big thing.

With a clear-headedness that I can only ascribe to the Holy Spirit in me, I said, 'Well, we'll pray for you in that, because if the sinus problem is preventing you from going to the very place where you love to meet with Father, then that is a big thing.' She pondered for a moment, and then smiled.
'I guess so, thank you!'

And I silently prayed for healing in her sinuses right there and then, and afterwards too.

The church wasn't full by any means, but it was a goodly number, and much more importantly it did feel like those present really wanted to be there, and that's better than large numbers who don't.

Ian & I were just so happy to be sat there with those lovely people, enjoying their company, and worshipping with them, giving deep thanks for Jesus, the cross, His death in my place so I could go free, and the love of Father.

It was all we could do to not sit and do our 'wonderment head shaking'. Although there were a few times it was impossible, and we gave in!

Communion.

Dougie welcomed and set the scene.
We sang psalms unaccompanied, led by the presenter at the front. It wasn't how I was used to, and I loved that.

One of the psalms was sung unaccompanied in Gaelic, I just listened with rapt attention. Josie beside me had a beautiful voice, and I stood and smiled as the musicality of the language itself as well as the truths being sung, washed over us.

Kenny's talk was once again just a beautiful call to come just as we are, and like an old song says, 'Jesus, take me as I am, I can come no other way, take me deeper into You, make my flesh-life melt away...'

And there followed three reminders for us all as we sat in that tiny village on the edge of the world...

There was the beautiful reminder of the extraordinary miracle that happened at the cross of Christ. He appeared in order to take away sin. My sin wiped clean, totally. Gone in the sight of Father, the one for whom it matters most. Do becomes Done, if our trust is in the Lord.

Oh, Jesus, thank you....

And there was the stunning reminder that Jesus, makes a second appearance, and right now, is in the presence of Father, interceding for us, with insider knowledge of what it means to live a human life in a broken world.

It struck me deeply that in the same way Ian & I had been calling out to Father on behalf of Neil, Lynnette, Beth and others, so Jesus brings our names to the Father. He prays for me. For you. That we won't be lost. He's doing it right now. He's been doing it from the moment you picked up this book and started reading. He's been doing it all your life. He knows, he hears, and he intercedes for us! He doesn't get weary of praying for you, ever. Thank you....

And finally, a crucial reminder that there will be a third appearance, at the end of all things when Jesus will appear again, and all will see and know, and He will call us HOME.

And when that moment comes and I walk with my new physical resurrection body into His presence, it will all be because of what He's done for me, not anything I could ever earn from Him.

Come home, folks. It's time.

We watched a lovely worship song video on the screens on the front wall while the elders prepared the communion meal.

And as the bread and wine were brought round to us, we all sat together in the quietness with a deep sense of gratitude that it's ALL about Him. The only thing we contribute to our salvation, is our sin, and a plea for forgiveness for it.

He does all the rest.

It's done.

'It is finished.'

Body broken & blood spilt.

We remember.

Bread and wine.

Now I can't quite explain why, but I do believe it was the most beautiful communion time I think I've ever known.

35

The 'More' of God – Lunches & Love

The service ended, although we didn't want it to.

There was mingling about, and a great buzz of chatter as the family did what families do, blether and catch up, and laugh, and wonder at things and share experiences and thoughts.

Oh, there was a really funny moment!
Do you remember that Christmas episode of 'The Vicar Of Dibley', when Rev. Geraldine ends up eating 4 Christmas dinners because she didn't know how to say no to all the invitations? Well, cue Barvas!

Ian and I were invited by 4 different families to have Sunday lunch with them! Had we been cunning and quicker off the mark, there was a window of opportunity there to eat like kings that day!

But thankfully, the first invitation had come from Joan & Dougie, so that made the apologising to subsequent invitations slightly easier. Although I did feel that spending time with Josie and Sammy would be lovely, so after sadly turning down their lunch invitation, I suggested to them that we could maybe pop over and have a cuppa with them after we'd finished in the manse. And the plan was made.

But how beautiful it was that such a welcome had been extended by the church family once again to two relative strangers in a campervan who had mysteriously arrived just a few days before!

The church building slowly emptied, I retrieved my boots from the porch, and after more chatter with folk on the gravel in front of the grey steps, Ian & I were finally the last ones left standing in the now quiet carpark.

There was something sad about seeing everyone depart up and down the main road, Cheery Colin being the last. We watched him walking north up the shallow slope on the opposite pavement – we would miss them all.

We wandered round to the rear of the building where a lovely house of similar colour to the church sat just a few yards away. This was the manse, where minister Dougie and his wife Joan and their son Jack lived.

We went in, and the kitchen was a hive of activity and delicious aromas as Joan prepared an awesome roast beef and Yorkshire pudding lunch! Kenny & Morag had been invited too, so the seven of us sat and ate and chatted and laughed, and shared stories and ponderings, some of which were hilarious, and some more weighty and thoughtful.

I glanced across to Ian at one point and we shared a knowing grin and hardly discernible nod of acknowledgement to each other. Words weren't necessary. We were pinching ourselves and enjoying the 'More' of God once again. What a blessing!

I thought back to the boathouse, the book, the sleeping years and the waking days, and marvelled that it had all led so quickly to here, eating delicious food in the wonderful company of some very precious people so far from our own homes, and yet feeling very much _at_ home.

Morag opposite me suddenly interrupted my revelry of thoughts and reminiscing with a gentle declaration again...

> _'I think there's something big around the corner for you, Chris.'_

And having delivered that, she navigated a neat forkful of roast beef into her mouth, turned to Joan at the end of the table and continued chatting. My own fork paused half-way through its journey to my mouth, and I just sat and stared.

I don't remember exactly, but I may have said a quiet, 'right, thank you!' to her, but she was already engaged in a different conversation. I slowly turned to Ian for some measure of reassurance that this was all actually happening and not some very long and unbelievable dream. With closed mouth he grinned, gently shook his head and carried on eating.

Later, Morag would explain that the sense of it was something of personal significance to me just in front of me that I might be about to walk into. So I hold that lightly but with seriousness too, as one does with the prophetic, and I wait for Father to make it clear in His timing.

Joan appeared like an angel carrying the most amazing looking cheesecake, my favourite dessert in the whole world! It was delicious!

Thank you, Joan & Dougie for your amazing hospitality, kindness and infectious joy! Your wonderful ability to host and welcome is truly a gift. Barvas is blessed to have you both.

Kenny & Morag needed to be getting back to Stornoway before returning for the evening service later, and they stood up to leave. I went round and gave Morag a hug and said, 'There's a beautiful lightness about you and your spirit that puts people at ease very quickly. Thank you.'

I didn't know it was a specific word from Father, or more of a general encouragement to a friend on the journey.

She and Kenny left the room, but a moment later she returned, and said thank you for what I'd just said as it echoed something of a meaningful prophetic word she was given some years back that it was good to be reminded of, adding 'Oh, and by the way, the thing around the corner for you, it's a GOOD thing!'

And having emphasised that, she darted away again, and they disappeared. She's an absolute gem!

That was the last time we would see them on our Grand Adventure.

They are a very precious couple, the kind of people you'd like to spend lots more time with, just listening to, learning from, and enjoying their company.

I hope one day again we will.
Thank you, Morag & Kenny.

36.

Tales & Tears

Shortly after, Ian & I also made our goodbyes, full of thanks for kindness shown by Joan & Dougie, and with a deep hope that we would be back again some time, and we sadly left.

We drove up the slope of the hill, and parked up outside a large bungalow, from where the view of Barvas, the machair and the coast was laid out in beautiful clarity.

Sammy and Josie welcomed us into their home, and we all sat in their conservatory. In the distance I could see the spray of the ocean once again rising in plumes like a geyser over the rocks under a grey sky.

Very apologetically, we explained that we only had about forty-five minutes, as we needed to be back in Stornoway for tonight's gathering at Martin's Memorial.
They were very understanding.

It was a strange thing, we didn't really know why we were there, but we'd felt that we should be.

Oh, their daughter Lorraine had gone for a run this afternoon, sinuses all good! Thank you, Father!

Something had aroused my curiosity, and so I asked Sammy how it was that he had come to faith just three years ago (an event he'd mentioned in passing, over cake in the back room of the church on Friday night) and he started to tell us the story.

I love listening to people's accounts of their journeys. It's like being given a precious gift, which you hold gently, turning it in your hands in wonder. Hearing others' journeying tales stirs you to keep going on your own, till the day all our paths will intersect and converge at the Great Homecoming.

So we listened intently as he told us something of the lead up to and him finally turning to Father and asking for forgiveness. There were key people in his life, one being Murdo who we'd not met but after the telling, we felt we'd like to one day. Apparently, Murdo had repeatedly cajoled Sammy, 'When are you Coming Home? Come Home!' They obviously had the kind of robust friendship that allowed for honest coaxing and challenging of one another.

And it had worked.
Three years ago, while in a marquee of a Faith Mission event in Barvas, Sammy had laid down his stubborn pride, and surrendered his life to Jesus, and his journey had taken an abrupt and beautiful turn.

The deep gratitude in his heart welled up in Sammy and Josie's eyes as they talked to us, interspersing Sammy's story with other moments in their lives together, some of them wonderful, some deeply harrowing. They are a couple acquainted with much grief, and yet determined to keep pressing into Father who they know without a speck of doubt is their All in All, and who will bring them safely Home.

It was very moving. The beautifully gentle and calm and honest way they shared their lives with us for that all too short a time was a real privilege to experience and left a mark on our hearts.

But time had caught us up. We needed to leave, so we prayed together for some moments, and at one point I looked up as Sammy thanked Father for all He'd done, and small tears were running down his face, tears of deep thankfulness. Ian and I had known some of those over recent days, as you know. It was a beautiful moment.

We got up to leave, and they invited us to please return sometime, and stay in their house with them. It wasn't just politeness, they absolutely meant it. They handed us a big hunk of cold roast beef wrapped in tinfoil as we left. So very kind. Thank you! Like I said before, there's quickly a deep bond between fellow journeyers.

And so we drove away from Barvas for the final time, with the ache of leaving in our hearts.

But also full of gratitude for all we had experienced there in that tiny village of scattered homes at world's edge, where the warmth of the church family had been lastingly imprinted on us and our lives made all the better for it.

Barvas, Oh Barabhais!

37.

Stornoway Songs

Hey reader, how are you doing?! Have you still got coffee? I expect the cake is gone now? Time for a biscuit then!

Chapter thirty-seven! Thank you and well done for getting this far! It's become a bit of an epic tome, I know. I only started out to write a few sides of A4, but as you now realise, it's turned into something way more than I thought it would ever be!

And maybe that in itself mirrors the way things had gone for Ian and me over the course of just the seven days we'd been away from home. The travelling days had become so much more than we had hoped for or imagined, by a long shot. A really, really long shot!! Out of bounds! And that is the way Father works, more than we could ever ask or imagine!

We drove back to Stornoway and had an hour on our pitch at Laxdale to sort ourselves out and get ready for the church gathering at 6.30pm. We were excited to be going back, really excited, and we had a few crackers and cheese, and then headed down to the town centre, parked in the long lane that runs up past the church building, and with djembe & guitar in hand, we went inside.

The Sunday evening service at Martin's Memorial church is a very informal gathering, and yet reverent and deeply meaningful. It's a lovely time of chat and worship, teaching, prayer and sharing of stories. The worship team were going through some songs when we arrived, and we sat at the side while they got themselves prepared and ready to lead.

The place filled up, packed with loads of teenagers, young adults and all ages beyond! We had lovely chats with folk round about us. There was a great buzz in the air, beaming faces and high expectancy, like before a gig is about to start.

But this was no performance.
This was ordinary people, longing to meet with our extraordinary God, worship Him, hear from Him, and then leave at the end that wee bit more strengthened to live for Him in all the tomorrows to come.

Like I said, high expectancy! Just how churching should be!

Tommy came to the front and welcomed everybody and explained how things might go for the next hour or so. He has this lovely boyish grin when he giggles which is highly infectious, and we smiled back as made us all feel welcome, delivered some notices and encouraged us to enter into Father's presence just as we are.

The worship band made their way to the platform, and we sang and worshipped for a while. It was really lovely to be there again, with another church family we were only just getting to know yet feeling like we'd journeyed with for years.

When it came to our part in the service, Tommy introduced us again, as there were many people present who'd not met us on the Wednesday night. And we did a short introduction to our journey and how we'd ended up here in Stornoway, and Martin's specifically. And then we sang.

Oddly I have little recollection of the moments that followed. Even my journal is foggy with the details. But I know we sang 'Prayer For The Nation' again. I know it was wonderfully received, and it so encouraged and stirred the church family. And knowing simply those facts is enough.

Ian & I then led another song called 'Sing To The King, Sing Praises', which is to the well-known and loved tune of 'Highland Cathedral'. Last year during the Boathouse gatherings I had written worship lyrics to it, and it's become a favourite of our church back home. I had used it as a soundcheck song on Wednesday night, and someone must have heard it and hence why Tommy requested it in his email.

Once again, it was taken up heartily by the Stornoway journeyers, and it gave me a warm glow of thankfulness to Father, to see something I'd penned last year, become a helpful way for folk to express praise to Father. So encouraging for me personally, and I hope a blessing to the church.

There was some more praise, and then Tommy did a great talk, another call to remember Jesus' return, and to live in the light and hope of that. Tommy is a superb communicator, and his love for Father and for the church is so evident in so much of what he says and also the manner in which he says it.

I don't know if the folk here on Lewis realise what an absolute blessing they have in Tommy & Donna, and Kenny & Morag. But I suspect and hope they do.

Now, during the whole duration of our time away, following the passing of Queen Elizabeth II on the 8th of September, we had been keeping sort of up to date with all the news about the upcoming funeral. It was a strange thing at times, we felt so far away and disconnected from the wider world, often with no signal anyway, but at 8pm that evening, Tommy hushed the gathering and we all joined with the rest of the UK and many other parts of the world, in a minute's silence of remembrance and respect for the Queen.

It was very special and led with great sensitivity and I was so glad that we were there for it.

The church gathering ended, and after lots of lovely chatting with folk, and being told by two separate people that I need to sing P4TN everywhere I go, we eventually with some sadness packed up our gear and headed back up the road.

At Laxdale we sat for a while in the van and pondered all that had occurred and how blessed we felt. We checked messages.

Neil was over the worst of the eye infection and might get home tomorrow!!! That was a huge Hallelujah! Tomorrow afternoon we would head south and begin the journey home.

We were so very tired then, and I'm hugely relieved to be able to tell you that for the first time since leaving Fife and Perthshire, sleep came quickly and deeply and blissfully undisturbed for the whole of the night!

Thank you, Father!

38.

The Bit Where We Say Our Goodbyes

Monday.

What a fabulous feeling to wake after such a deep slumber!!

We got up and breakfasted and checked the clock. We were to meet Tommy down by the church to pick up a couple of boxes of 'Sleeping Giant' books to take home. But in the messaging back and forth to arrange this, it was decided to meet later, after the televised Queen's funeral.

So after checking out of the site and a short chat with Gordon and thanks again for all they had done for us, we drove down and parked up in Stornoway harbour carpark beside the ferry terminal, just round the corner from the church. We made a coffee and watched the funeral service on my tablet.

Wasn't it just a beautiful service?

Full of the light of Christ, stunning worship music and stirring words and readings. I felt very uplifted by it, and sad too, that such a bright beacon of faith has passed.

We prayed that the words and songs and testimony would cause ripples of new faith around the world. It was watched by so many millions globally. So many people, like us, saying their goodbyes.

We met Tommy, collected the books, and he told us that he would be doing a book tour in November and would be coming to Perth! This was great news! And lovely to know as we were saying our goodbyes to him, that we would all meet up again soon!

And so we left.

It was 1.20pm.
Our ferry crossing from Tarbert back to Skye was at 4.20pm.

After refuelling, we drove unhurriedly southwards, passing across the high moorland. The sun was hidden behind clouds, but it was still bright and dry, and the roads were quiet of traffic.

We were brimming with thanks and praise.

We should've felt sad to go, but oddly in that moment, we didn't. We felt excited for the weeks ahead and what the outward ripples of our journey might be.

At one point as I was thinking about being back home again, I felt a check in my spirit and a Holy Spirit whisper,

'Hey, don't think this is over yet!'

I wondered what that might mean.

As moorland gave way to the great rising mountain of An Cliseam at the southerly end of Lewis, we prayed for family and friends, and then once again for our own humility in all that was happening, so vital in the sharing of the stories when home, and whatever happened beyond that.

We passed by landmarks and features that we remembered from days ago, but it genuinely felt like weeks ago we had passed this way going north, and simply years since we'd taken the ignition keys from Derek and begun our travels!

We came into Tarbert, and discovered they were just opening the barrier at the ferry terminal, so we went through and took the first place in the right-most boarding lane.

We had well over an hour to wait so we nipped up to a wee shop on the main street above the carpark and bought newspapers and some chocolate and then just relaxed in the van.

I finally caught up with my journal writing and Ian pondered and read.

39

The Leaving of Tarbert

We boarded the ferry just after 4pm and stood up on the deck as before.

Not long after we pulled away from Tarbert pier, Ian spotted a pod of dolphins off to the south, amongst the archipelago of small dark islets which dotted Loch an Tairbeairt. They were circling a shoal of fish as seabirds screeched above them.

The sky was a beautiful collage of banded horizontal layers of greys as we picked up speed and forged our way through the dark sea. I looked back and gazed at the mountains behind Tarbert, rugged and monochrome and dark below the twilight sky, and whispered deep prayers of thankfulness...

> *Father, thank You...*
> *For the journey, for the process.*
> *For the tears, for the joys.*
> *For the surprises, for the songs.*
> *For the people, for the bread and wine.*
> *For the love, for the laughter.*
> *For the sights, for the company.*
> *For the change in us, deep change.*
> *For the recognising of Your voice,*
> *And for Your gentle touch...*

And as the ferry trundled on towards Skye, its engines sounding a low rumble that thrummed through the hiss of the bow-wave and spume, gazing back I watched the hills of Harris fade into the distance.

Clouds hid the peaks and a delicate haze descended on the islands till I could hardly distinguish sea from land or land from sky.

And as the islands vanished along with the boat's distant wake behind us, I prayed that the experiences and changes wrought in us by beautiful people and God-moments wouldn't. I prayed that all the lessons learned, and the memories of people and places we've loved would remain.

> Vivid
> And clear
> And bright
> And close by
> Even with the passing of time.

'Goodbye Harris, goodbye Lewis!', my heart waved.

I almost didn't dare to, but tentatively I asked Father,

> 'Will we ever come back again?'

The whisper came back quickly,
    with a glint in the eye, and a smile…

> 'Sooner than you know!'

So with deep relief I smiled too, turned through one hundred and eighty degrees and pointedly aligned my gaze across the bow to the east, to where new adventures were calling us forward.

In my mind's eye, Father was out in front, striding with all the purpose and determination of the One who knows all things.

And we were following on behind, like the two Skuas that glided effortlessly behind in the lee of the ship the entire way from Tarbert to Uig, faithful in their desire to stay close in its wake at all times, until they made landfall and a safe harbour.

Let it be so with Ian and me.

Please, Father.

Following on faithfully and close,

toward whatever lands You lead us next.

40

'We're Not Finished Yet' - Broadford

The journey from the harbour in Uig down to Broadford passed very quickly. We wondered about finding that same spot on the Elgol road to overnight in, but then just half a mile before Broadford, Ian said, 'This'll do!' and we pulled over into a layby overlooking the rounded island of Scalpay on the far side of a narrow sea loch.

It was starting to get dark, and following our usual parking-up routine, I made us a lovely Thai curry. After watching me, and since returning home, Ian has blessed his own family by making one. They were impressed. I taught him well!

After eating, we got a fresh energy to pray again. So we prayed for Neil, that there would be no need for his eye patch and he would be back home and healed. For Lynette that she would have the voice to be able to sing on Sunday at church.

I also messaged Beth to say we're still praying for you. She messaged back this exact sentence:

'Today I feel secure that He's got all this covered'

We were abruptly halted in our tracks.

Everything stopped.

Our minds raced back to just yesterday morning, sitting in the van in Barvas church carpark, and Father's voice to me, telling me not to pray at that moment for Beth and others...

> *'...Don't be in prayer for them in this moment.*
> *I've got them. They're covered...'*

I love that!
I love that SO much!
What He had said to me in Barvas, he had also communicated clearly to Beth. The same words.

It's just mind-blowing.
And totally humbling.

And as you grasp something of just what is going on here, that the One who set the universe in place and the galaxies spinning, also knows and cares deeply for ordinary you and I, and sends us songs and eagles at exactly the right moment, and speaks to us and invites all of us into this unbelievable adventure with Him....

...Well, there are no words really.

But lots of shaking of heads and exhaling deeply!!

And grinning!

And worship.

Yes, lots of worship.
The All of me to the ALL of Him!

I messaged Beth to tell her!

She was buzzing!
She had a deep peace and deep sense of being held and loved.

Thank You, Father!
You are unbelievable!

But we believe You!

As we'd been driving south through Lewis earlier, I'd had this doubtful wondering whether it was all over now, and the God-moments were finished. But He had that covered too.

'We're not finished yet', had come the gentle still small voice.

And we went to sleep that night with a clear sense that there was way more to come, and that the weeks and months ahead would be just as speech-stopping, perhaps more so than the last eight days.

If indeed that were possible.

And we slept deeply once again.

41.

The Return

Tuesday.

How does one describe the returning from a pilgrimage, a grand adventure like the one we had?

The air is tinged with the sadness of the leaving.
There is some fear that what was experienced will be lost.
There is some uncertainty and concern about whether the connection with Father can be maintained.

But...
There is also hope. And for Ian and me, with each mile closer to home, a growing certainty that the things to which we're called in the 'ordinary days', will also be a grand adventure, an almost seamless continuation of the journey, albeit without a campervan (perhaps?!).

In all honesty we don't think very much of the days ahead will be 'ordinary'. We think 'ordinary' has been swept away by what we've seen of Father and His extra-ordinary weaving of the tapestry we're all part of.

Sam and Frodo returned to the Shire at the end of all things, changed by their experiences and journey and moments of undoing, fear, hope, courage and love.
Things would never be the same again.

And we too had been changed by the journey.

So we were heading home today.

It was a bright morning, and the sun was glancing through high wind-smoothed clouds. Crepuscular rays fanned out and touched the beautiful landscape like vast spotlights on an enormous drama-filled stage. The heather, dead bracken and dark green of the broom and gorse bushes on Scalpay across the water were lit beautifully.

Looking at it made me smile out loud.

After eating blackberries in yogurt kindly foraged by Ian (the blackberries, not the yogurt) (never eat foraged yogurt!), we headed back over the high sweeping arch of the Skye Bridge and down into Kyle of Lochalsh, and we became mainlanders once more.

And we prayed on...

...as we drove past the stunning Kintail mountain range, Invergarry, Spean Bridge where we turned left up to Laggan and then down the slowly winding A9 to Blair Atholl, Pitlochry, and Perth.

It was just impossible for us to go any length of time without whispering out some deep expression of thanks and love to Father. And asking for Him to seal in us all that had happened, and asking for courage and humility and His clear leading for the days ahead...

And finally, back to Derek's house.

....

Oh Derek, how do we begin to explain when you ask us, 'How did it all go?'

Ian's wife, Rose is there to meet him on the pavement, and I busy myself in the van to give them some space.

We empty the van of baggage.

But not all the baggage.

For some unhelpful baggage had been left behind, thankfully, so thankfully,

At Ceann Hulabhaig, at Barabhais, at Martin's Memorial Church, places where mending and the lifting of weighted blankets, baggage of sorts, had occurred.

I pack my car; the van is returned to Derek's safe keeping.
What a blessing that wee home on wheels was for us!
Thank you, Derek & Anne. So much.

And it's time to part ways.
I give Ian a long hug.

There are no words, and I feel a welling up of tears, which I try and disguise with the wiping of an imaginary speck of something from my glasses. We'll speak soon.

And I turn and get into my car where I try and work out where on earth the ignition is, it's been centuries since I was last sitting in it.

Actually, just eight days.

But what an eight days!

I set off on the forty-minute drive back to Crieff.

It's the first time I've driven with no-one beside me in 860 miles, and I miss Ian immediately.

But I have the ever-present company of Father, by His Holy Spirit right beside me and in me, spurring me on and reminding me of the days passed, and of the promises of what's ahead.

That's a very good way to journey.

The best way.

All the way HOME.

42

Ripples

The next morning, I woke up in the cottage with a measure of disorientation. And after realising the campervan hadn't suddenly expanded and changed colour and become filled with possessions I didn't recall ever taking with me, and that I am actually home again, I lay in the quietness and pondered, and shook my head slowly and smiled.

'Good morning, Father!'

I got up, and coffee'd and began a conversation with Father as I pottered about.

I was quickly struck with a wave of fear and dark doubt and panic looming over and through me, that it was all going back to pre-waking days and the whole adventure had been a one-off, a blip, an island poking above the waters of Ceann Hulabhaig that had for a time shone in the sun but would now quickly be submerged and disappear beneath the rising tide of normality, routine and ordinariness. It wasn't nice.

I was unprepared for this dark attack of doubt. It shook me, and so I pressed in, and continued praying, calling out Father! I worshipped and praised and thanked, and paced around the cottage, until, sometime later, like a receding fog, the doubts left, the shadows fled, and a peace entered the room, and I felt the quickening of the Spirit again. I breathed deeply and slowly, and calm flooded my heart. It was ok. It was just the battle. I should've known and been ready. I hoped I would be from then on and in the days to come.

Right now, as I'm writing this final bit, it's been nineteen days since we came home. And sadly, dear reader, dear friend, our journey together is drawing to a close.

It's been lovely having you with me as I've written and pondered how to begin to explain all that's happened in the past year. Thank you for getting this far and staying the course! We do need to part ways shortly, but first, let me bring it all home by talking about the ripples.

So much has happened in the few weeks since our return home. And as is becoming normal now, I'm not quite sure where to start, it could be a whole other book!!

I suppose, first-off, I wrote this! I've not written a book before, but over the course of nineteen days, it has poured out of me in a way I could never have imagined! And that is all the Holy Spirit's doing. And my prayer, along with the goosebumps that accompany it, is that reading this will have been an encouragement to you, and any others that may happen across it in the future.

You see, as we travelled the north-western part of Scotland, we were increasingly aware that our journey was being watched from afar by friends and family, and church folk, and even by many of the friends I have made in care homes and other places I regularly sing in. Particularly in the four weeks prior to leaving, during gigs I was sharing some of the plans and excitement about going on this journey to have space and time to pray and be still and explore.

So it shouldn't have come as a surprise that during and on our return there were many, many requests from people to hear the stories! One day last week, someone asked me, 'How was your trip, then?' I just stared and exhaled and didn't know how on earth to begin.

What would you have said, had it been you?

It wasn't just a trip. It was something momentous for us that changed Ian and me forever, hence the need to write it down in a way I hope folk can relate to and be drawn into and have those same moments of 'Oh my!' that we regularly had. There are some specific people I know I'd like to give this story to, but maybe it might go wider than that?

While we were praying on the return journey, I did have a picture come to mind of concentric circles of ripples spreading out in a deep pool. But in contrast to how things are in the natural, these ripples were actually *gaining* height and strength as they travelled outward, not dissipating. They collided with other ripples from other journeyers and became stronger with crests of foam at the tips. And I remember being excited, and goosebumpy as I thought about where all this might lead. Oh Father, YOU know!

As the church gathered on our first and second Sundays back, it was fabulous! We met with Neil, he was out of hospital, and while his eye is still not at all right, he didn't need it removed, there's no eye-patch now, and we pray on!
Thank you, Father!

We also saw Lynette, and SHE SANG!!! Yes, Lord!!! So glad she did too, she has a beautiful voice, and a gentle spirit that is such a blessing in a worship team. And her condition is improved but not healed, so again we pray on!

We've had a chance to share some of the God-stories while churching, and some folk are eager to hear more, and we're more than happy to oblige on that one!

Last week I popped by to see my dear friend Beth.
We had tears together, and two hours of chatting God things, and praying and calling on Father to keep reviving us and make us overcomers! She gave me permission, in fact requested that I write a bit more about her, so you know. This puts the message I sent her on the Saturday morning from Barvas that I told you about in a bit more context...

A while back, she developed an alcohol addiction. It was so very hard for her and the family. And while she goes months and months without giving in, sometimes she has a moment of failure, and she falls and is covered in deep despair and deep shame. It happened on the day we set off, and I'm so glad we had the time and space to pray consistently and often for her, holding her up, and praying the truths of who she is in Christ over her, across the miles.

No shame. No guilt. Because of Jesus, because of the cross. Do becomes Done.

We pray on, but Beth's story is so encouraging – though there's struggle, she presses on, and she IS an overcomer. Present tense. Her witness to Father amongst her colleagues and friends is so powerful. Father doesn't wait till we're perfect and have everything sussed before He urges us to tell our story, He'd be waiting till we're no longer breathing. Instead, he loves to use our brokenness and low times and struggles – it's then HIS glory shines through, and he cherishes our frail worship in those times as pure gold. So precious in His sight.

Thank You, Father, thank you for dear Beth, the overcomer.

My wonderful mother, Wendy, who was closely following all our travels, and praying for us is also now going through her own waking up in her hearing of Father's voice over the past days. She's so excited! And it's amazing to see and hear! We speak most days, and it's all God-moments we're sharing! She feels lighter, and a weight has lifted. Thank You, Father, so much!

Oh! Let me tell you of an AMAZING moment last week again... (Have you got time?) I was singing with some mostly elderly people in Perth. It's a place I go to regularly and they know me well. On the way along the A85 I was praying for wisdom and sensitivity to that fine line between sharing a story and going beyond what the context of the gathering is about. I didn't want to get that wrong, and make staff or visitors feel uncomfortable. It wasn't a church gathering.

But here's what happened...!!!!
They wanted to know all about the journey, so I was telling them all (twenty-five in the room) about us seeing the Eagle glide down in front of us, having just been singing '...And as I wait, I'll rise up like the eagle...' and I described something of the emotion of that God-moment. And then I went on to sing another usual song. After it, one of the elderly ladies calls out,

'Would you sing the other song!'

At first, I wasn't sure what she meant.

'Would you sing the eagle song, the church one?'

There was a moment where I just checked myself. I wasn't entirely certain. So I just ask the group, 'Well it's a church worship song, is everyone ok with that?' There are no complaints but a great deal of encouraging nodding and eagerness and expectant waiting.

So I sing 'Lord I Come To You', and during the last chorus I look round the room, and the lady who asked, and her neighbour are sitting with an arm raised up in worship. It was a beautiful moment. At the end there were some tears in the room, and you could've heard a pin drop.

Ripples.

I visited Lynsey and her husband in the last few days too, that was lovely to catch up. I'd prayed for her back on Luskentyre beach, do you remember? Again, it was great to all chat and pray together. Some tears, and lots of hope, laughter and calming faith for the days ahead. Father is good at growing that in us! We talked with much jaw-dropping about the tomato plant (you won't know about that!) - but that's definitely a story for my next book! Watch this space!

And so it goes on.

Ian has had some wonderful conversations with friends and family, and there's more stirrings and excitement. Recently, he and Rose met up with Donald and Chris-Ann, a couple from the Barvas church family who were on their own campervan journey south, and they had some lovely hours together, during which, Donald handed Ian a book – 'When God Came Down', the story of the North Uist Revival of '57-'58.

I didn't even know that was a thing! I'm looking forward to reading that story! And by the way, not to freak you out or anything, but Rose's watch stopped for thirty minutes then carried on during that meeting too. No words. Or understanding about that at all. We just let it settle. And shake our heads. Some things are a mystery, and that's ok.

So it seems that, in some peculiar way, our journey and stories are stirring up others to listen out and look upward and outward, and seek Father, and want to journey more closely with Him too. Which is just amazing and overwhelming and humbling, and another beautiful answer to prayers prayed both during the Donut Days and while travelling. Thank You, Lord.

This morning I had a lovely message from a dear friend who I'd sent some chapters to. He was reading them on a plane heading abroad, and he'd had some tears, and a growing hunger and stirring. And there are loads of others on a similar journey too, and we're linking in with them more, and sharing the stories, it's so exciting! Next month Tommy is doing a book tour around the five biggest cities in Scotland, and we'll get to some (or all!) of those and meet other journeyers!

Ian and I have met up numerous times since coming home. We've sat in the car, and in our homes like we did before and have carried on where we left off, praying and listening and worshipping, and being very, very grateful, and asking some tentative questions about what next, Father?

He's got it covered. And we're keeping close.

Ian has a message he's written for you too, I'll place it here...

Hello readers,

God woke me up, He woke Chris up and I think He is going to wake up a lot more people too. The time for sleeping is over. He woke me with a book, a friend (who sticks closer than a brother), and a journey in a campervan. Who knows how He might waken you up? But this is certain, He will do it with love, patience, kindness and gentleness which He poured out to Chris and me through times between us and Father and times between us and those whose paths we crossed on our journey.

Maybe our paths might cross somewhere on your journey? He is waiting with His arms wide open ready to take you on that journey that will be beyond your wildest dreams.

So here is the apostle Paul's prayer to the people of Ephesus. I pray it for all of you, especially if God is stirring you from your slumbers.

Ephesians chapter 3, verses 16-21...

I pray that out of his glorious riches he may strengthen you with power through his Spirit in your inner being, so that Christ may dwell in your hearts through faith. And I pray that you, being rooted and established in love, may have power, together with all the Lord's holy people, to grasp how wide and long and high and deep is the love of Christ, and to know this love that surpasses knowledge—that you may be filled to the measure of all the fullness of God.

Now to him who is able to do immeasurably more than all we ask or imagine, according to his power that is at work within us, to him be glory in the church and in Christ Jesus throughout all generations, for ever and ever! Amen.

Thanks to all you wonderful people at Martin`s Memorial Church and at Barvas Church. I hope you have some idea of the enormous part you played in God`s plan to restore me and Chris.

But most of all thank you my loving heavenly Father.

This is the time.

Ian

Oh! And just before we go, here's some last-minute news to tell you... This week we got an email inviting us back to Barvas to be involved in some more things there with the church family early next year! HUGE GRINNING!!!!! The delightfully unexpected 'MORE' of God again!

The returning 'Sooner than you know' has come to pass already! Isn't that amazing!?

So I'm very thankful for so many things that have happened in the past twelve months...

For Richard, the boathouse, and the lovely welcoming Loch Leven Church family. For Tommy and his book, 'Sleeping Giant'. For Ian & Rose, and their treasured friendship, which is such a huge blessing in my life. For the waking. For the wonderful church family at Martin's Memorial in Stornoway. For the dear friends in Barvas, and an invite to return there. For all the beautiful places and moments we've had.

...And for the ripples that continue and grow.

But over all of those, for God himself, Father, Son and Spirit, who has orchestrated all this, and saved, woken, stirred, fed, guided, whispered, led, prodded, mended, blessed and changed me. In the sleeping times AND in the waking times. Nothing is wasted. He's been there all along and is with you too. Close enough to whisper to. Try it now, go on.....

And you, dear friend, you've now become part of the journey, because you're reading this.

And whatever the days ahead hold for you, be they calm or chaotic, my advice is this: seek Him, spend time with Him, worship and walk and run with Him.

Find other like-minded journeyers and hold them close and have adventures together.

Travel very lightly, shed some baggage, ask Father for mending moments, be bold, tell your own stories amongst friends, family, colleagues, in schools, pubs, homes, shops and in the streets...

Go and MAKE RIPPLES!

Huge ones!

All for HIM!

And just to finish; while this is the story of Ian and me and a journey we went on, I hope by now you've realised,

...it's actually HIS story.

Father.

It's all about You.

Our spot for the first night on the Elgol Road, Skye

*The Card Lynsey sent us before
we left, 'A God' Adventure
awaits!*

Leaving Skye

The Quiraing, Skye, looking north

The Quiraing, Skye, looking south

Ian on Luskentyre Beach, Harris.

The rocky road from Rodel to Tarbert

Loch Ceann Hulabhaig – the mending & the eagle!
This picture was taken by a man who was in the layby near us as we
were leaving – Ian asked him to send it on to us!

The beautiful Kneep beach (Traigh na Beirigh), Lewis

Looking south-west across Ardroil Bay, Lewis

Stone circle, Callanish
(Photo Ian White)

Ian in Barvas Church

Me praying on the steps of Barvas Church (Photo – Ian White)

Me at Ness, at the Butt of Lewis (Photo – Ian White)

'Don't pray now!' – the cows in the field at Barvas

The leaving of Tarbert

Praying for Lynsey on Luskentyre beach, Harris (photo Ian White)

Thank You!

Thank you to the many folk (islanders & mainlanders alike) mentioned in this book who gave their generous permission to have a wee bit of their stories told, as their lives intersected with ours.

Thank you to all those who gave invaluable editorial suggestions and comments as I wrote (Mum!) which helped both the accuracy and flow of the narrative.

Thank you to my friends and family, for always encouraging me and for praying us along on our journey.

And thank you to Ian, my fellow journeyer.
I'm so very glad our lives are interwoven.
Here's to many more journeys,
until the Great Homecoming at the last!

If this book has helped you in some way or you would like to comment, do contact me...

awakeningsandripples@hotmail.com

Printed in Great Britain
by Amazon

11228652R00102